The Last Dog

When the world gets crazy, finding serenity in dogs, Spirit, and nature

HOWARD G. OLSON

ISBN: 1545082766
ISBN 13: 9781545082768

This book is dedicated to my father, Calvin "Big Bear" Olson, who nurtured my love for the natural world, and gave me life. And to my yellow Lab, Casey, who taught me how to accept love, and saved my life.

My heart leaps up when I behold
A rainbow in the sky:
So was it when my life began;
So is it now I am a man;
So be it when I shall grow old,
Or let me die!

—William Wordsworth, "My Heart Leaps Up"

TABLE OF CONTENTS

FOREWORD

The Last Dog is an extraordinary book. Howard Olson writes the way he has lived: from his heart, with deep connections to the natural world, the spirit world, and his ever-present and always happy Labrador dogs. I know this because we are neighbors. For thirty-five years, I have lived—as the crow flies—a wet marsh, an oak ridge, and a forty-acre cornfield away from him.

For ten of those years, we served together on boards and commissions in the rural Wisconsin township where we live, trying to do what we could to protect the land in which we have become rooted. Much of this book is about the importance of preserving the natural world around us as a place where people can find peace and refuge from a world going crazy. Howard has always fought hard to protect and preserve the land and water in our township. His enduring respect for the land and traditional Native American spirituality are woven into the fabric of many of his stories.

The stories in this book are about the sometimes difficult task of finding serenity in our lives. In these pages, we join Howard on a journey through life's joys and challenges, starting with childhood, passing through early adulthood and the confusions of middle age—and finally coming back home as the journey ends. *The Last Dog* encourages us to take the road less traveled, no matter how difficult life gets.

Through Howard's words, you can discover your own voice, connect with the land on which *you* live, and realize that you are following your own precious life path, not anyone else's. Enjoy *The Last Dog*. Celebrate the journey.

—J. Roderick Clark, Editor & Publisher, *Rosebud* magazine

Over the last fifty years, a predictable pattern has developed—the crazier my life gets, the more time I spend in the woods with my dogs. It's a coping strategy that I didn't consciously adopt; it has just happened. I am fortunate that the circumstances of my life have allowed me the freedom to retreat into the healing mystery of the natural world. Deep within me, there is a small, still voice; I call it Spirit. The voice beckons me when it's time to escape from the chaos and noise of the world. I believe that the woods, Spirit, and the six Labrador retriever dogs that have shared my life have helped me stay off the psychiatrist's couch and away from mood-altering medications. For all of this, I am grateful beyond words.

During my thirty-five-year career as a professor at the University of Wisconsin-Whitewater, I wrote a textbook, and many articles that were published in professional journals. At the same time, I was also writing stories about my annual canoe trips into the Canadian wilderness and traditional week-long bow-hunting trips to northern Wisconsin with my father and his friends. I also wrote a series of six stories called "The Urban Wilderness," which was about discovering and disappearing into secret places within the city limits of my hometown, Madison. These stories were about how, in the solitude of the late-night and early-morning hours, one could find peace and connect with Spirit in the woods and on the waters of a crowded city.

I wrote the textbook and the journal articles primarily so that I would eventually get promoted to full professor. I wanted this promotion mainly so that I could have more free time to be in the woods—walking with Spirit, and my dogs. The dogs seemed to know this. Fortunately for me, the dean and the chancellor of the university never figured it out.

When I was a boy, perhaps seven or eight years old, I would often ride my bike five blocks to a place called Murphy's Creek. With the legs of my blue jeans pulled-up to my knees, and using my cane pole for balance, I waded across a spillway and squirmed under a fence into the University of

Wisconsin Arboretum, a four-hundred-acre urban wilderness. The land was owned and managed by the university as a natural research area. I remember the rush of excitement and freedom I felt being in that secret place, where surely no other white person had had ever been!

One day, a German shepherd dog that lived in a nearby house, wandered into the arboretum and we spent most of the day together. I could hear the owner calling for his dog, but I successfully alienated the dog's affection and loyalty by sharing parts of my baloney sandwich with my new best friend. That day, I fell in love with dogs, and the affair has lived on and grown throughout my life.

Also around this time, my brother, three sisters, and I would periodically put on a carnival in my parents' backyard during the summer months. Our large extended family, and many of our neighbors, would walk through the midway of "Howie's Big Show." My sisters would entertain, for no charge, by twirling batons and performing acrobatic tricks on the swing set. I charged customers who were curious to see "the world's tallest midget in captivity": five cents to view my older brother sitting in a tent wearing a Halloween mask.

But my favorite way of making money at the carnival was telling fortunes. I loved it when the crowd laughed. As I moved into the fantasy, vivid and colorful pictures appeared in my mind, and I would act out the scenes and put the pictures into words. I encouraged them to ask questions of the other characters described in the story, and I would channel the words of these imaginary people. It was fun having the license to talk to my relatives and parents in ways I would never have dared outside of the safety of make-believe. It was during those times that I first knew I was born to be a storyteller. And I've been at it ever since my days of telling fortunes in "Howie's Big Show."

At the age of ten, I discovered what I wanted to be when I grew up. My fifth-grade arithmetic teacher decided one day that it would be a good idea to segregate the class into two groups. The achievers would sit on the right side of the classroom, and the underachievers would sit on the left side. My heart pounded, and I was dizzy from the dread of being embarrassed as she announced the seating assignments.

The relief I felt when she announced that I could stay seated on the achiever side of the room quickly evaporated as I saw the humiliation and shame on the faces and in the body language of my friends and classmates who were ordered to the left side. The concept was to provide motivation for the underachievers, but I can only imagine the hurt that dreadful experiment must have inflicted on those tender and innocent children.

One of my friends who had been labeled as an underachiever was excellent at multiplication, but he struggled with division. One day, as we practiced arithmetic with flash cards, I was able to show him how both procedures involved three numbers, and if you knew the answer in multiplication, the answer in division was one of those same three numbers. He got it, and he zipped through the division cards without a mistake.

The next day in arithmetic class, the teacher started him with three multiplication cards, which he nailed. She then moved into division. After twenty perfect answers, she waved him to the right side of the classroom. I watched as he walked proudly to the achiever side of the room and took the seat next to me. As we shook hands under the desk and smiled knowingly at each other, I knew that I wanted more of this; it's called "a teacher's high."

My teaching style at the University of Wisconsin-Whitewater was to create interest and action and drama by telling stories instead of always lecturing. The students became characters, and played parts in the stories, just like what happened many years before in "Howie's Big Show." My style and philosophy of teaching were "outside the box," to say the least. Reading off old power point slides, and disseminating information for memorization was simply not my style. But something must have been working in my classes, as I experienced hundreds of teacher highs, and won the all-college excellence in teaching award four times.

This book is the culmination of a lifetime of teaching, living in the woods, seeking Spirit, telling and writing stories, and loving dogs.

The entire first paragraph of Scott Peck's best-selling book, *The Road Less Traveled*, is simply three very wise words: "Life is difficult." This great truth has played its hand in my life, and in the lives of every person I have known. The purpose of *The Last Dog* is not to suggest methods or strategies to avoid or escape the difficulties that Scott Peck writes about, but rather to give them meaning as necessary components of a life well lived—a life that has value and can bring insight and wisdom to fellow travelers.

When my world is going crazy, it is always partly because I don't like what is happening, and I feel powerless to change or control whatever is upsetting me. The other part of the craziness is the fear that swirls around me, as well as within me. There are hundreds of varieties of fear that cause us humans to instinctually fight, flee, or freeze. They might be necessary for survival, but none of them is a pathway to serenity and contentment.

Much of the craziness we see in the world and feel in our beings comes from the stories we create and play over and over in our own minds— eventually coming to believe they are true. Some of the world's oldest wisdom traditions and enduring philosophies teach that the genesis of most human suffering is trying to fix the unfixable, create certainty out of uncertainty, make permanent what is always changing, and/or change the things we don't have the power to change. *God, grant me the serenity to accept the things I* cannot *change, the courage to change the things I can, and the wisdom to know the difference.*

The stories in this book are based on actual events and experiences. The lessons learned are universal; they are here for all of us to discover and use on our journey through life.

With dogs, Spirit, and nature in our lives, miraculous healing and transformative experiences can occur. The craziness of the world will give way to the order and serenity that no human power can create. There will be no need to fight or flee from anyone or anything, or try to change the reality of what is. We will experience a knowingness that we really are connected to the bigness of the whole. Oneness will shift from being a concept to becoming part of our bones. When I am locked into the fear-based stories I have created in my mind, the priceless gift of serenity is unattainable. *Grant me the wisdom to know the difference.*

Yes, these are big promises, but they will materialize if we let go of trying to control how the world works and allow the flow of the universe to work. If we do this, life will indeed become less difficult and less crazy. My hope for all of us is that we can connect with the Spirit of dogs, the Spirit that dwells within us, and the Spirit of the Earth, and live our lives with more serenity and peace.

Howard G. Olson
Contact me at:
olsonh1967@gmail.com, or
www.thelastdog.net

ACKNOWLEDGEMENTS

A special acknowledgement to my six children: Sam, Casey, HR Clancy Girl SH, HRCH Little Maggie MH, Cody Ann MH, and Lefty MH. You had bad breath, were excellent hunters, and all of you have found your way into this book. I learned so much about life and love from you. Thanks for sharing your sweet and beautiful dog lives with me.

When I was four years old, my father introduced me to the woods and the waters where he and his friends hunted and fished. More than anyone, he fanned and nurtured the ember of love for wild places that I was born with. Thank you, Dad, for taking the time and having the patience to take your boy with you into the magic of the natural world.

I had many older male mentors who showed me the ways of the woods and taught me lessons about life. Thank you all. Special thanks go to Bob Williams, who was important in developing my early connections to the Earth and the spirit world. The first story of this book, "The Swamp Buck," is dedicated to his memory.

I am blessed to be friends with Native Americans who still practice tribal traditions and ceremonies in their daily lives. Thank you for so generously sharing your knowledge and understanding of how the natural world creates the foundation for your cultural connection to the Spirits, and the Earth Mother. Your insight and wisdom is found in almost every chapter of this book.

In Montana, I have been welcomed into a community of trout-fishing outfitters and guides. For the past twenty-five years or so, these men have taught me how to fish and navigate the wild rivers of Montana. Thank you all, especially Earl James and Big Sky Anglers for your friendship and generous sharing of your passion—fishing wild trout in places where experiencing God just comes naturally.

Finally, thanks to my editor, Peter Perry. We met through a mutual friend, and have become good friends while working on this project. You have helped me to better understand the English language, and your encouragement kept me going forward when I was getting tired.

And to those who read some of my stories and said, "You should publish this stuff"—well, here it is. Enjoy the read.

PART 1: THE JOURNEY BEGINS

We could never have loved the earth so well
If we had had no childhood in it.

—*George Eliot*

When I was young, my father often told me stories about Mother Earth, the loving protector who watched over her children. She provided food, a place to live, and wisdom that would be helpful to her children when they grew up. As a five-year-old boy, I was intent on gripping my bamboo fishing pole, and staring intently at the red-and-white bobber, unaware that I was already gleaning lessons from the natural world. By age ten, I was fishing trout with dry flies, and at twelve, I walked into the grown-up world of my first deer camp.

I loved being in the woods and on the water with my father and his friends. It gave me a sense of being a part of the group, and I wanted desperately to contribute something of value so that they would invite me back. My father sparked my love and respect for the natural world, and the values I learned as a boy have served me well throughout my life. The following two stories describe the connection and excitement and joy I felt when I was hunting and fishing. They also reveal painful feelings of inadequacy and of not fitting in that were, and sometimes still are, lurking in my emotional shadows.

THE SWAMP BUCK

The Child is father of the Man.

—*William Wordsworth, "My Heart Leaps Up"*

"Should I get more wood for the fire?"

"No," came my father's patient reply. "With the moon full, the bucks will be rutting early in the morning."

The bedtime message was clear, but sleep was impossible as I lay wide-eyed in my sleeping bag, listening to the campfire talk outside the tent. My father and his hunting buddies retold the story about shooting arrows at the old swamp buck that was chasing does around the oak knob.

Bob, Bill, Hal, and my father, had become good friends while shooting archery in a league during the late 1940s. The war had sent them to the far reaches of the world. Now their common love for the woods and wild places had brought them together once again to bow hunt for deer during Wisconsin's November rutting season.

Morning at last did arrive, and as my father strung our lemonwood bows, Bill approached.

"Where are you and the boy hunting this morning?"

"We don't want to get in anyone's way, we'll go where you aren't."

"Why don't we go to the oak knob?" I asked excitedly. "Maybe I can kill the old swamp buck with my sharpest arrow."

Father and I waited until the other three hunters had made their decisions and headed toward their morning deer stands. Hal was hunting the ridge, while Bill headed to the "grocery-store stand," and Bob took the long walk to the oak knob.

On the way to our deer stand along the creek, my father explained that the older guys should get the best stands since I was only twelve years old, and new in camp. I needed to behave myself, or I wouldn't be welcomed back. The prospect of being left at home with my sisters during future hunts brought a cold lump to my throat, and I steeled myself against the creeping fear that I had offended the older guys by speaking up for the oak knob stand.

The Morrison Creek stand was my worst nightmare. As we slogged through the peat bogs, my four-buckle galoshes leaked, and eventually freezing water poured over the tops. By the time we reached the island of tamarack trees, I was soaked and muddy from the knees down.

A lightly used deer trail ran ten yards from the rotting stump I knelt behind. My father was stern: "Don't move, face into the wind, and keep an eye on that buck rub, as he might come back to make another. I'll be in those birch trees."

"Maybe the swamp buck rubbed that tree," I speculated hopefully, as my guide disappeared into the woods.

The frost sparkled like millions of prisms as the first rays of sunshine broke out of the eastern horizon. For three hours, I sat motionless, staring at the buck rub, and feeling my feet going numb. Dare I risk moving to dump the water out of my galoshes, I wondered. Would wringing out my socks and tennis shoes be just another rookie violation that would keep me out of deer camp forever?

By noon, my father's nickname of "Sitting Bull," referring to his legendary patience on a deer stand, was taking on epic proportions. With cramped legs and bare feet, I cautiously approached the birch trees, desperately fearing that my movement might chase any deer away from the area.

Upon seeing my purple and wrinkled feet, my father predictably asked, "Why are you walking around in the woods with no shoes on?"

"It's easier to sneak up on the deer for a good close shot," I responded, dropping my soaked and muddy footgear at his feet.

After sharing a salami and lettuce sandwich, an apple, and a can of beer, we sat together, searching for any sign of deer. Somehow my suffering seemed to diminish as I sat with my father in this alien place. If a deer happened to appear, I now knew the older guy, not the boy, would be the one to take the shot.

A barred owl pumped out its eerie call, as the long shadows of evening crept across the bog.

My father slowly turned his head and whispered, "It's the golden hour; stay alert and get ready."

This was it, the golden hour, when the swamp buck chases the does around. How I wished I was back at the buck rub, since he would surely come back there. I slowly knocked my sharpest arrow and hooked my left index finger over the varnished cedar shaft. My heart pounded, just at thinking I could be the hero of the camp, and of the older guys if I killed the swamp buck. They would tell campfire stories about me, for sure.

The owl sailed silently from its perch to do some hunting of his own. My whole body shook on the verge of hypothermia, but I dared not complain or ask to leave.

Finally, as the moon rose behind the tamaracks, my father turned on his stool and proclaimed, "Well, that's it for today."

Upon our arrival in camp, the mood was deadly serious, as Hal and Bill filled their Coleman lanterns with white gas and looked for a rope.

"Get your tracking shoes on, Bob hit the swamp buck on the oak knob just before dark," reported Hal.

My tracking shoes were on, wet and muddy, but I felt the excitement stir deep in my soul as Bob acted out the drama of the big buck's approach, the shot, and the wild crashing of the wounded deer running up and over the oak knob into a tag-alder swamp.

Bob took his recurve bow and quiver of wooden arrows, as he and I and my father followed the lantern light to the oak knob. Toilet paper marked a brown oak leaf that had a spot of bright red blood on it.

As the lanterns slowly moved up and over the knob, I heard someone say, "Good blood, he's lung shot and shouldn't be more than another hundred yards."

My head swirled at the thought of the swamp buck being just another hundred yards. What a campfire story this will be—and I can tell it!

"Stay here and don't move," my father commanded. "We've lost the blood trail."

My heart fell to the ground, as the lanterns slowly disappeared into the tag-alder swamp, and I sat alone on a stump at the edge of the oak knob.

The moon was high, and it seemed as if the trackers had been gone for hours. Fear of having to sit alone on the stump until morning brought tears to my young eyes, and I stood up to search hopefully for distant lantern light. While staring into the moonlit shadows of the tag alders, something shiny and mysterious-looking loomed forty yards down the hill.

Wiping away the tears with the sleeve of my flannel shirt, I looked again, as the moon reflected a light that magically drew me off the stump. I ran down the hill, and to my amazement, there lay the swamp buck, dead in the moonlight.

I opened my mouth to yell for the trackers, but no sound came from my dry and tightening throat. Dropping to my knees, I felt the moisture of his still-open eyes and the sticky blood on his extended, limp tongue. I felt the smooth coldness of his enormous antlers and counted each of the twelve points. My hand ran along the sleek hair of his neck to a dark spot on his shoulder. My index finger entered the warm hole in his shoulder; the shattered rib bone felt sharp and dangerous. Putting both hands on the swamp buck, I wanted him to be alive again and to get up and run away. I didn't want the campfire stories to die with the swamp buck there on the oak knob. His stories needed to live on for me and others to tell.

The tears returned and rolled down my face as I said goodbye to the swamp buck and slowly walked back to my stump. Death became real to a twelve-year-old boy that night. So did a deep respect for all living things, and what it means to participate in a creature's death by hunting.

As the dimly lit lanterns approached my stump, gloom and dejection hung heavy among the trackers. I could hear Bob mutter, "I'm just sick about this; it makes you want to quit hunting."

"Get the boy and let's get the hell out of here," snapped Hal, "I hope the brandy bottle is full."

At the stump, my father patiently explained that sometimes in hunting, animals that are wounded get away. Even with sharp arrows and good shots, sometimes these things happen. After many moments of silence, my small, faltering voice finally came.

"Bob, I know where the swamp buck is," I whispered, in a voice choked with emotion.

The only sound was the low hiss of the failing Coleman lanterns as the four men stared down at the boy sitting on the stump.

"Follow me, I'll show you," I said, regaining command of my voice.

As we circled around the dead deer, no one spoke until Bob lifted me up in a big hug.

"Oh my God, thank you!"

There were handshakes, and slaps on my back, and shouts of joy as the disbelief turned into celebration. Chattering and speculating about how they had gotten off the blood trail, how much he weighed, and where to hang the deer continued until Bob found his metal deer tag.

Handing me the tag, he said, "Here, the swamp buck is our deer, you put the tag on his leg."

My hands trembled as I slipped the tag through the slit in the deer's gambrel. When I felt the tag snap shut, I knew my fate as a hunter was sealed. I knew it would be a life sentence, and I've loved every moment of it.

The next year, and for years to come, when Bob told the story of the swamp buck, he asked me to tell parts of it, and always, he made me the hero of the story. While he talked, I felt I finally belonged—that I fit in. I was no longer the boy who had to be tolerated, but rather one of the guys, who had value—and some campfire stories of his own to tell.

Author's Note:

This story is dedicated to the memory of my father, Calvin (Big Bear) Olson, who brought out my love for the Earth and natural things; of Bob Williams, who took the time to gently welcome me, as a twelve-year-old boy, into the hunting tradition; and of Bill McCormick and Hal Schimming, from whom I learned many things while sharing countless campfires. Although all of the original four "rut hunters" in this story have passed on, sometimes I can still feel their spirits, and vaguely see their shadowy images sitting motionless on their deer stands in the failing light of a cold November evening.

MONSTER ALLEY

Do not dwell in the past, do not dream of the future,
concentrate the mind on the present moment.

—*Buddha*

The grease-stained pizza box was upside down on the floor next to his mattress. The bed had no box spring, and it was positioned in front of a nineteen-inch portable television. ESPN was starting its early-morning coverage of the final round of the PGA golf tournament. Chris opened his left eye and watched the first pairing tee off, while his right hand groped for his Copenhagen tin among the pizza crusts and empty beer cans scattered around his mattress.

The small one-bedroom apartment in West Yellowstone, Montana, was perfect for Chris's lifestyle as a trout-fishing guide. He had tried to follow society's road map to the American Dream, but for Chris, that dream had never come true. Marriage, the suburban home, and the suit-and-tie corporate culture felt like death by suffocation to him.

Chris was a free spirit, and he knew it in his bones. The mountains, rivers, and open places were the drummers calling him to the dance of life. To deny their call would mean a cruel life sentence of trying to please other people.

The pinch of Copenhagen was generous that morning as Chris settled in for a long, relaxing day of watching sports on television. As Tiger Woods lined up a birdie putt on the second green, the caller ID indicated that his boss at Bud Lilly's fly shop was on the phone.

"Good morning, Chris. I got a really old guy here, a Calvin Peterson, who wants to do a walk-and-wade trip today. Are you available?"

"I've been on the river for sixteen days straight, and I've just 'assumed the position' to watch golf on TV, so I'm pretty comfortable. How old is this guy?"

"He's old enough to be your father, and he just wants half a day. Take him someplace easy and close. He'll meet you at the shop about noon."

"You got it, buddy."

Chris stumbled out of bed and headed for the shower.

■ ■ ■

The last time Calvin Peterson had been in West Yellowstone at Bud Lilly's fly shop was on August 15, 1959. He and his 10-year-old son, Kenny, needed grasshopper flies, and Bud Lilly's always had the best selection in town.

"I want the big ones with white hair on top, so I can see 'em in the riffles," Kenny told the sales clerk as he dug for money in the pockets of his faded blue jeans.

August was the month when the Peterson family took its annual two-week trout-fishing vacation to Montana's famous Madison River. For months prior to the trip, Kenny saved money he earned from doing chores and cashing in returnable soda pop bottles for three cents each.

"Someday I'm going to be a trout-fishing guide, and tie my own flies from the deer and turkeys I kill," Kenny assured the clerk as he paid for his six grasshopper flies. "Here's the lucky one. I'm fishing this one in the fast water below our cabin."

■ ■ ■

Forty-seven years later, Calvin's tired blue eyes were once again gazing at the large assortment of grasshopper flies on display at Bud Lilly's. As if suddenly awakened from a dream, Calvin jumped as the smiling guide stuck out his hand.

"Hello Mr. Peterson, my name is Chris. Let's go fishing!"

Chris's strong grip engulfed the old man's frail and trembling hand.

Chris had left his old Ford Bronco idling behind the shop. He patiently helped the old man onto the running board and into the truck.

"This town's really changed since I was last here in 1959. I'm 84 years old, but it seems like just yesterday that my son Kenny and I were leaving Bud Lilly's to fish trout on the Madison River."

The old man silently stared out the passenger window at the mountains flanking the Madison River Valley.

Breaking the uncomfortable silence, Chris inquired, "Does your son Kenny still fish trout?"

The old man ignored the question, folding his arthritic hands in his lap.

After many miles, putting his weathered hand on the guide's forearm, Calvin asked, "Do you know where Mrs. Powers' resort cabins were before the 1959 earthquake?"

"Sure I do. The quake shook loose half a mountain, which slid into the river and dammed it up. The cabins floated around in what's now called Quake Lake. Later, when the Army Corps of Engineers removed some of the mud and rocks, the water level went down, and the cabins are scattered along the old riverbed."

"I know. My wife, my son Kenny, and I were staying in one of the cabins on the night of the quake. I remember the roar of the wind, and the cabin tipping toward the river. We followed other panicked guests to higher ground, back from the river. I remember how the moon became hazy, and then totally disappeared as huge clouds of dust filled the air."

Chris now realized that his client really didn't want to go trout fishing. Calvin's only interest was finding the old Powers cabin.

Late that afternoon, Chris and Calvin finally made their way to where the Madison River widens and flows into Quake Lake. The old man remembered that on the day before the quake, he and Kenny had borrowed

Mrs. Powers' inflatable raft, and fished along the rock cliff on the west side of the river.

■ ■ ■

The grasshopper fly floated naturally along the face of the granite cliff.

"Great cast, Kenny!" beamed Calvin.

At the tail end of the float, just as Calvin was about to coach Kenny in recasting more upstream, the glistening hook-jawed mouth of a large brown trout had appeared in the slick water. The trout inhaled Kenny's fly, and disappeared into the swift current.

"Set the hook!" Calvin yelled.

"I got him! He's on!" Kenny shouted, as the raft started to spin out of control, heading toward the menacing rapids below the cliff.

"Don't horse him; he's a monster!"

The fish charged upstream, digging deeply into the fast current, and then made a hard run back downriver toward their tiny raft and the dangerous rapids.

"Keep your rod tip high. Give him line," Calvin instructed, as the trout shot out of the water, giving father and son a teasing glimpse of its beautiful red-and-black spotted flank.

"He's a monster. He'll never fit in the net," Kenny sputtered.

His nine-foot fiberglass fly rod arched and strained against the trout's powerful run to the rapids.

■ ■ ■

The old man's chest was heaving as he caught his breath and turned toward Chris, who sat riveted in the driver's seat. And then, with an expression of disbelief, Calvin pointed straight ahead.

"That's it! Right in front of the truck, Chris. That's the cliff, and those are the rapids where Kenny caught a 21-inch brown trout on August 17, 1959."

Calvin recounted how the small raft had capsized in the rapids, and how he and his boy beached the trout on a shallow gravel bar.

"We were both soaked and covered in mud—and laughing! We lost the net, our creel, and Mrs. Powers' raft, but together we got that trout. I can still hear Kenny's voice, as he lifted the trout from the river, held it over his head, and yelled over the roar of the rapids, 'We got him, Daddy!'"

Tears rolled down his leathery face, as the old man remained caught in his exciting and vivid memory.

"I can still see Kenny's shiny wet face with a big smile, river mud smeared in his hair, and his small hands gently releasing the trout back into its Madison River home. He said, 'I'll see you next time,' as the big fish slowly finned sideways and disappeared into the shadowy depths of the Madison River."

Struggling to form words with his trembling mouth, the old man recalled, "I remember both of us crawling up that steep bank right in front of us, and standing next to that flat rock. Kenny dropped his muddy fly rod, hugged me around the waist and said, 'Daddy, I'm glad we're here.'"

Chris helped Calvin out of the truck. They stood silently next to the flat rock, listening to the roar of the rapids, and watching the water slip past the rock cliff on the opposite side of the river. Calvin swept his right hand across the scene in front of them.

"It was forty-seven years ago today, and I can feel Kenny's spirit here with us now!"

About a hundred yards upriver from the rapids, the remnants of some old dwellings lay scattered along a sandy point of land.

"Take a look at those buildings" Chris said, handing Calvin a pair of powerful binoculars. Bracing his elbows on the Bronco's hood, he scanned the broken and scattered remains of cabins on the river's western shore.

Stopping suddenly, he focused intently on a small collapsed log cabin.

"That's it! I see it! I'm sure that's the one," he shouted. "That's the cabin we stayed in the night the quake hit—the day Kenny caught his big trout."

Opening the back door of the Bronco, the old man excitedly pulled out his ancient chest waders and a six-foot hickory wading stick.

"You've got to get me across the river Chris!"

Calvin fumbled with the worn-out red suspenders as he struggled to get into his patched and tattered wading boots.

"Help me down this steep bank. We can cross the rapids where the water is shallow. Hang on to that end of the stick. Let's go!"

Calvin cinched the wading stick's leather strap around his left wrist, and the two struggled and inched their way down the steep embankment to the river.

"Here's where Kenny beached his big trout!" yelled Calvin.

His voice softened.

"That was some day, Kenny. You and me and the trout—right here."

With a guide's eye, Chris surveyed the angry rapids, and then looked back at the old man. Bent forward on his stick, tilted and frail, Calvin's eyes burned with determination and resolve. To Chris, the whole picture was crazy, and he didn't even know why the 84-year-old man with leaky waders and an old stick needed to cross this treacherous stretch of the Madison River. But Calvin was the client, so Chris was determined to try.

With a shrug and a deep breath, Chris grabbed the wet end of the wading stick and found a solid foothold between two large rocks upstream from the old man. From one solid and braced position to the next, Calvin Peterson and his guide slowly and methodically moved into the swift and noisy rapids. They used hand signals and head nods to communicate when to move, and when to rest.

Chris's strong arm and back muscles ached as he strained to hold himself, and the weight of the old man, against the river's relentless force. Calvin felt cold wetness on both of his legs as some of the square rubber patches loosened and gave way to the current.

"My right boot is filling with water," Calvin yelled as he struggled to navigate over the slippery rocks and boulders.

Fear gripped him as the river's powerful force drained the remaining strength from his unsteady legs. The swift water boiled up around his leaking waders, and panic spread across the old man's face. Glancing back at the Bronco, and the shore they had just left, Calvin was sure they could retreat back to their last safe place, but he was paralyzed with indecision and fear.

Chris knew that if Calvin weakened and succumbed to his fear in the middle of the crossing, he would be swept downriver and would most likely drown. They had to move soon, either backwards or forwards, but further delay was no longer an option.

Looking back one last time, Calvin nodded to his guide, and took one more tiny step toward the opposite shore. The leather strap of the wading stick cut deeply into his left wrist, but fear and adrenaline made him oblivious to the pain. His bent arm jerked upward, and then down, fighting to maintain balance as he and his guide slowly felt their way across the slippery riverbed.

"You can do this. Keep going!" Chris urged as the old man slogged forward.

With only a few yards to go, the fast water caught Calvin's dangling boot leg and sucked both men into the torrent of white water running along the western shore of the river. Chris, in wading sandals and shorts, grabbed the red suspenders just as the old man's head disappeared under the foamy white water, and kicked hard to get him to the surface.

A bald eagle in a nearby cedar tree curiously turned its white head to watch the pair splash their way to shore.

"We made it! You just saved what little life I have left in these old bones. Help me out of these damn waders. Let's build a fire and dry out."

Calvin dug into the pockets of his soaked pants, producing a waterproof plastic bag containing two envelopes, an old pipe, Sir Walter Raleigh tobacco, a jackknife, and a lighter.

Chris started a fire.

Sitting directly in front of the old man, he said, "Okay Calvin, it's time you tell me exactly why it was necessary for us to risk our lives to get to the remains of that old cabin."

The old man went silent again as he drew a deep inhale from his time-worn pipe.

"Open the big envelope in that plastic bag and read me the letter."

Smoke from the fire mixed with the old man's tobacco smoke and swirled into the cloudless Montana sky, as Chris read the letter out loud.

November 28, 1968
Dear Mr. and Mrs. Calvin Peterson:
I regret to report that The Secretary of the Army has classified your son, Pfc. Kenneth G. Peterson, as Missing in Action.
On November 19, 1968, Pfc. Peterson was on a reconnaissance mission, deep in enemy-held territory, east of the Ia Drang River in the Central Highlands of South Vietnam. The ten-man team of eight American and two indigenous soldiers were detected by a company of North Vietnamese soldiers. Being outnumbered 15 to 1, the American-led commandos called for air and artillery support while retreating to a narrow crossing on the Ia Drang River.
Pfc. Peterson volunteered to defend the river crossing against the attacking enemy. Firing his M-60 machine gun, Pfc. Peterson held off the enemy, while the rest of the team safely crossed the river to establish a defensive position in the thick jungle on the opposite riverbank.
During the maneuver, tactical air support arrived and laid down heavy suppressing fire, killing many of the advancing enemy soldiers. Pfc. Kenneth G. Peterson was last seen running along the east bank of the Ia Drang River, firing his .45 caliber pistol at a large number of pursuing enemy soldiers. For three days after the battle, rescue teams searched the area, but were unable to locate any sign of Pfc. Peterson.
For his gallantry and bravery beyond the call of duty, Pfc. Kenneth G. Peterson has been recommended to receive, in absentia, the Silver Star.
Sincerely,
Col. R.C. Harris
1st Battalion, 12th Cavalry
U.S. Army

Chris sat silently as the old man removed the medal from the smaller envelope, laying it gently on his flattened left palm. Rays of afternoon sunshine reflected off the Madison River and Kenny's Silver Star. Calvin looked skyward.

"This is where your heart and dreams are. Welcome home, Kenny."

The old man's head dropped, and his worn, bent fingers slowly closed around his son's medal.

The guide and his client sat quietly, staring into the fire. Calvin's mind wandered back in time, thinking about Kenny's grief-stricken mother, and wishing she could be with him. She had placed candles in the windows of their home every night for two years after her son had been classified MIA. She could not bring herself to extinguish hope by having a memorial service for her missing boy, although many family and friends encouraged her to do so. During her final year, Mrs. Peterson rarely left the house. She died in her sleep three years after Kenny disappeared.

When Kenny went MIA, Calvin had quit fishing. He was waiting for Kenny, and it just wasn't the same fishing alone. Over the years, his spirit of adventure faded. Visits from Kenny's army buddies became less and less frequent. Although Calvin longed for closure, thoughts of a service for Kenny at the veteran's cemetery seemed hollow. He had kept the last chapter of Kenny's life story unfinished for forty-seven years.

■ ■ ■

A small pile of warm ashes was all that remained of the fire. Using his wading stick, Calvin stiffly pulled himself into a semi-standing position. The guide silently followed his client along the riverbank as they slowly navigated their way to the ruins of the old Powers cabin.

The partially collapsed log cabin appeared to have grown into the stony hillside. Young alders and fireweed grew in dense clumps around the weathered structure. A chipmunk scurried under the tilted floor, as Chris and the old man stopped outside the cabin's door.

"There it is Chris. Can you read it?"

He ran his index finger over a dark carving in a large log at the bottom of the cabin's door. Squatting beside Calvin, Chris read the deeply carved inscription, "8-17-59 K.P. 21in Brown." With the same jackknife that his father now carried in his pocket, Kenny had memorialized his monster trout on a log in Mrs. Powers' cabin—forty-seven years ago.

Kneeling by the cabin door, Calvin opened Kenny's jackknife and brushed his right thumb across its sharp stainless-steel blade. Chris perched on a large rock, watching as Calvin carved. The old man dug into the log resting above the one with his son's inscription. He worked with care as he cut each letter and each number deeply into the still-solid wood. A deer mouse poked its curious head through a crack in the window sill, and watched with shiny black eyes as Calvin determinedly chiseled.

Chris moved from his perch on the rock, and standing next to Calvin, read the freshly carved message out loud:

> *Pfc. K.G. Peterson*
> *12-23-1948 to 8-17-2006*
> *Welcome Home Son*

Tears gathered in the guide's eyes and rolled down his tanned cheeks. Calvin put his arm around Chris's shoulder, and they stood reverently staring at the new marker, just above Kenny's timeworn announcement of his 21-inch trout.

Calvin picked up his wading stick, and moved to the large rock that Chris had been resting on.

Jamming the stout hickory stick under one edge, he ordered, "Chris, help me lift this rock. We're not finished yet."

When one side of the great rock was lifted off the ground, Calvin rolled a smaller rock underneath it; to support the big rock's enormous weight. Chris watched as the old man used his wading stick to scrape and dig a shallow depression under the propped-up rock. Calvin opened the letter from Colonel Harris and laid it in the depression. On top of the letter, he placed Kenny's jackknife, the Silver Star, and finally, the old pipe—his companion for the past forty-seven years.

The old man pulled on the supporting stone while Chris flattened his back against the huge rock; groaning as he lifted its enormous weight.

"Okay," Calvin yelled as he pulled the support clear. Chris instantly released the rock, memorializing parts of Calvin and Kenny's past in that special place.

The guide's extended hands helped the exhausted old man to his feet. As the two friends stood, connected by clasped hands, Calvin turned his face skyward, and recited the eulogy he had been saving for so long.

> *My dear son Kenny, I can feel your nearness. The wait has been so very long. I have seen you in my dreams, knowing that you, too, were waiting for me. Your shadow, on the horizon of my mind, has kept me anxious and paralyzed. Now my life goes on, my son, so that I may be the fountain of your new beginning, as well as of my own.*
>
> *So ride the wind, to that far-off place that still holds your pain. Release the hurt that keeps you there, and open wide to this place again. Welcome home my son. I love you, dearest Kenny, and that will never change.*

"When you float by this spot with your trout-fishing clients, might you tell them about Kenny's 21-inch brown trout—just to keep him alive through his stories?"

"I promise I will, Calvin, and I am naming this stretch of the river Monster Alley, in honor of Kenny and his big trout."

"Thank you, Chris. Monster Alley—I like the sound of that."

The sun slipped below the horizon as Chris and Calvin looked across the river to where the Bronco was parked. Both men knew that crossing the river again was impossible, and the prospect of spending a cold night in Mrs. Powers' collapsed cabin sent a shiver of fear up Calvin's spine.

Chris could just make out the faint silhouette of the eagle perched in a cedar tree next to the river. Before he could comment on how odd it was for an eagle to be fishing so late in the day, the old man suddenly yelled, "Hey, over here! Help! Over here!"

Waving their arms and shouting, the pair had caught the attention of a father and son who were fly fishing from a green wooden canoe. The young boy stopped casting while his father skillfully paddled the canoe toward the stranded men.

"How's fishin'?" asked the boy.

While Chris searched for a reasonable answer to why they were standing, without fly rods, on the opposite side of the river from the parking lot, the boy interjected, "I had a big one on in the riffle upstream. Almost broke my new rod! We'll get 'im tomorrow, right, Daddy?"

"Maybe, just maybe," nodded the boy's father, who smiled knowingly at the two men standing on shore.

The boy and his father happily agreed to ferry, first the old man, and then his guide, across the river to their truck. As the canoe entered the current, Chris overheard the old man talking to the boy.

"Someday, try fishing down by that rock cliff above the rapids. Many years ago, my son Kenny caught a 21-inch brown trout on a grasshopper fly—just like the one you're using."

Wide-eyed, the boy exclaimed, "A 21-incher? That's a monster, right Daddy? Do you think the one I lost in the riffles was bigger than 21 inches? Can we come here tomorrow and fish by the rock cliff, Daddy—maybe?"

Calvin sat in the dark, waiting for the canoe to return with his guide. The evening star reliably appeared in the southern sky, and the river sounded friendly and welcoming once again. The old man smiled, as he fumbled in his pants pockets, searching for the pipe that wasn't there anymore. He thought back on the events of the day. At last, life was good again—he was free, and Kenny was home!

After dropping Chris off, the green canoe floated downstream to where the boy's mother waited patiently to pick them up. Over the sound of the river, Chris and Calvin smiled as they overheard the boy ask, "Daddy, can we go over there by that rock cliff? Mom won't mind waiting if we fish just a little longer."

Chris helped the exhausted old man up the steep bank to where the Bronco was parked. Pausing by the flat rock, they stared into the darkness, where the old Powers cabin lay, with new markings carved into one of its logs. Chris had never before hugged a client, but he wrapped his strong arms around his cold and frail friend.

"I'm glad we came here, Calvin. Let's go home."

As Chris helped the old man into the Bronco, he asked, "Calvin, would you like to go fishing with me tomorrow? I have the entire day off, and it'd just be you and me. We could drift and fish the Madison River in my boat."

"Ya, boy. Let's go!" Calvin's voice rang with new excitement and enthusiasm. "We got to hurry. Bud Lilly's closes at 9 p.m., and I need some grasshopper flies with white hair on the top."

As the truck sailed past the turnoff to Quake Lake, the old man asked, "So, what stretch of river do you think we should fish tomorrow?"

Chris contemplated the options for a few moments.

"How about Monster Alley?"

Author's Note:

This story is dedicated to my father, Calvin, who patiently helped develop my love and respect for the Earth and wild places. Also, many thanks to friends in Montana who have taught me lessons, shown me secret places, and generously shared their skills; so that I may be a better trout fisherman. And finally, to the soldiers who were wounded, killed, or who disappeared (MIA) in the Vietnam War, and to the families of those soldiers.

"Monster Alley" is based on fact and on personal profiles of real people.

Chris, who guides on the Madison River, embodies the lifestyle of free-spirited fishing guides.

Calvin Peterson possesses many of the characteristics, behaviors, and speech patterns of my late father, Calvin Olson. In August of 1959, my family was en route to camp at the Rock Creek Campground. Our truck developed mechanical problems in the Badlands of South Dakota, and the trip was delayed by two days while the truck was being repaired. During that time, the Yellowstone Earthquake loosened a mountainside, which slid across the Madison River and buried the Rock Creek Camp Ground. The "bad luck" of the truck breakdown saved the lives of the seven people in my family.

The personalities of both Kenny, and of the young boy in the green canoe, are drawn from my own experiences as a ten-year-old, fly fishing with my father.

The Yellowstone Earthquake did occur during the night of August 17, 1959, and Mrs. Ann Powers' Resort Cabins did float in the waters of what is now called Quake Lake.

Montana's Madison River was named by Lewis and Clark, and its rapids and riffles are legendary blue-ribbon trout waters.

And finally, Bud Lilly's fly shop is now Big Sky Anglers.

PART 2: SOCIETY'S ROAD MAP

The biggest adventure you can take is to live the life of your dreams.

—*Oprah Winfrey*

The path to a happy destiny—the American Dream—is taught to us from an early age by parents, teachers, and other adults. Television, movies, internet, magazines, and other media continually reinforce the message. We are told that we should graduate from a prestigious college and get an important job that pays well. And since the list of material things that we'll need to be happy is endless, more money is always better, no matter where we have to live or what we have to do to get it. An attractive spouse, a fancy house—bigger is always better—and well-behaved, bright and beautiful children are also important components of the happiness trip ticket. Social status and prestige, as evidenced by what we drive, how big our boat is, where we golf, and our community leadership positions in the schools, churches, and government are also important parts of the equation.

Following society's road map, and staying on its narrow highways is difficult, especially for those who fall behind and don't measure up. America esteems the "winners," and the "losers" will have to look on in envy or anger. Life is difficult for everyone—"winners" as well as "losers"—and there is no way to buy out of this universal truth.

My house is over one hundred years old. It's located in a beautiful natural setting; there has been no spouse; all of my children have had four legs and bad breath, and were excellent hunters. Some parts of my life have been excruciatingly painful and difficult—as were the lives of good friends who had made millions by the age of thirty-five.

During this part of the journey, you will meet and know the dogs that made my life easier and more fulfilling than it would have been without their wonderful company. And you will feel the pain and grief as they say goodbye and leave on a new journey of their own. You will meet the dog that, without question, saved my life during my dark night of the soul.

My life did not follow our society's road map, rather it took the road less traveled. I will share with you the wisdom of the natural world that I learned from a Lakota Indian elder; what a red-shouldered hawk taught me about the futility of trying to create and control alternative realities for other people; and the importance of finding one's own True Self."

GOOSE MUSIC FOR CLANCY GIRL

Gentle and forgiving, Clancy brought me the gifts of peace and serenity.

Only ten days into our traditional month-long trip to the trout rivers and mountain camps of Montana, Clancy Girl, my fourteen-year-old yellow Labrador retriever, suffered a stroke while swimming in the Bighorn River. Her cloudy, tired eyes told me that her time was close, and that she wanted to be home on Cedar Lake to watch the geese fly—just one more time.

The winding road up the west slope of the Bighorn Mountain range was steep, and the sign read Sheridan Wyoming 126 mi. Clancy's broad yellow head lay on my right thigh; her breathing was steady and rhythmic.

"How ya doin' old girl?" I asked, as she shifted her stiff arthritic hips to get more support from the passenger seat. Although the muscled and powerful hindquarters of her youth had slowly surrendered to the weakening atrophy of age, her strong Labrador spirit and fierce hunting desire had kept her in the field well beyond what could ever have been expected.

■ ■ ■

I remember how her aged eyes had gleamed as we prepared to leave on this adventure. Loading the truck with camping equipment, kayaks, guns, and fishing rods always presented a time of high drama and anticipation for Clancy as she lay near the tailgate. Her eyes would plead and her tail would pound the ground in the hope of getting an invitation to "load up." After the final piece of gear was stowed, I would squat in front of Clancy, look into her hopeful eyes and ask, "Do you want to go?"

As a young dog, she would rocket into the back of the truck and excitedly bang her tail in appreciation against the topper's window. Recently, her eyes still shined and her tail wagged as she carefully walked up the carpeted dog ramp, and lay down on her cushion in the back of the truck.

■ ■ ■

The drone of Harley Davidson motorcycles on Interstate 90 signaled the end of the annual bikers' rally held in Sturgis, South Dakota. The Dakotas are waterfowl country, and I remembered some of Clancy's retrieves during the years we duck and goose hunted together on the Great Plains.

I recalled when she was a young dog; anxious to retrieve a big drake mallard, she had pulled me face-first into a frigid pothole as she lunged against the nylon leash that was fastened to my belt. Another time, my poor shooting had resulted in only breaking a wing on a tough old canvasback duck. With Clancy in hot pursuit, the duck swam and dived his way far out into the whitecaps of a large North Dakota lake. After twenty minutes, having lost sight of both the duck and Clancy, tears filled my eyes as I sat on a rock and sobbed for the loss of my friend. Surely she must have become exhausted and drowned while stubbornly refusing to give up on retrieving the duck.

Staring out into the cold wind and foamy black water, I felt alone and hopelessly sad. I wondered if the joy of hunting with my beloved Clancy Girl was worth the risk of such a profound and painful loss. As I stood to take the lonely walk back to the truck, far down the driftwood-littered beach, like a mirage, appeared the beautiful sight of a proud Labrador coming home after a difficult retrieve.

I suppressed the urge to run to her, happily blew the come-in whistle, and wiped away the tears with the sleeve of my flannel shirt. As she sat to deliver the tired and bewildered duck, I wrapped my arms around her big wet neck and felt the love for Clancy surge through my heart and every fiber of my being. Others had their families; Clancy was my girl—my family.

■ ■ ■

The early-morning drive through southern Minnesota went quickly as Clancy slept through the loud country music that was keeping me awake. Rest stops were difficult, as Clancy had to be lifted from the front seat and carried to the dog exercise area. Never before had she ever refused anything to eat, but even canned dog food was unappealing in her weakening and confused state. Although her condition was rapidly deteriorating, I remember that her thick tail thumped the seat and she licked my face when I lifted her earflap and whispered, "Clancy, you're my girl and we'll always be together."

Finally, the Mississippi River, and the last leg to home. My right hand wandered over the softness of Clancy's ears and scratched the bony underside of her lower jaw. The road sign read Black River Falls 98 mi. My mind wandered back to the traditional November bow-and-arrow deer hunting trips that Clancy and I had been on for each of the past fourteen years.

I thought about her first hunting trip to Black River Falls when Clancy was only nine months old. I had locked her in the front seat of my new Toyota pickup truck while I took a deer stand on an oak ridge about half a mile from the road. With both front paws planted firmly against the passenger window, Clancy yipped her disapproval of being left behind as I disappeared into the woods. As darkness began to settle into the forest, I heard the crunching of oak leaves as an animal approached the area. I excitedly knocked an arrow, and my eyes strained to see the deer in the failing evening light. Closer it came, and finally, my heart melted as I watched Clancy make one last circle and excitedly bark at the base of the tree I was standing in. The sliding glass window behind the extended cab of the truck had provided the escape hatch she needed to track me down so that we could be together.

■ ■ ■

It was 6:00 a.m. when we turned onto our home road and drove past our fields of switchgrass and big bluestem. HR Cedar Ponds Clancy Girl SH died that morning, looking over the fields, the marshes, and the lake where we had hunted and explored together over the fourteen years of her life. The old dog and I lay together in the grass for three hours before I reluctantly called the veterinarian.

Flocks of Canadian geese noisily flew over us on their way to feed in a nearby wheat field. Gentle and forgiving, Clancy Girl had brought me the gifts of peace and serenity, and I was happy that she left with the sweetness of goose music in her ears.

Author's Note:
"Goose Music for Clancy Girl" is related to another story in this book: "Clancy's Gift" is about the healing gift of forgiveness that preserved a wonderful friendship.

MAGGIE, A SPECIAL YELLOW LAB

*Nobody else wanted the runt dog with a bad eye and
deformed jaw, and now I'm glad they didn't.*

She wiggled up the veterinarian's long arms, trembling with the excitement of being touched.

"Sure is a happy little girl, considering all of her medical problems. But nature's way is to weed out the weak ones, and before you get attached..."

He stopped in midsentence, and I quickly lifted the squirming yellow Labrador puppy from his arms. After watching her fight valiantly for the past six weeks to stay alive, I could not allow this little dog be "helped" to die.

On her own, she was working hard to beat long odds in the game of life and death. For me to let her life end with a poison-filled syringe on a cold stainless steel table was simply not in my heart. At that moment, I knew that the runty little pup with the runny eye and irregular jaw was not only going to make it, but was going to be a very special dog—if she was given the chance.

The vet helped me load the nine-puppy litter into the back of my pickup truck. Cedar Ponds Clancy Girl, their mother, eagerly jumped into the front seat and sat next to me. Her raised ears and gleaming eyes pleaded for a trip to the bank, where Milk Bones magically come out of a steel drawer.

During the following week, people who had made deposits on the puppies came with their families to pick out their newest best friend. The pick of the litter was a stocky male, who was named Roscoe by his new owners. One by one, the selections were made. Eventually, the only puppy left was the runt female with all the medical problems.

The man who had the ninth selection said he liked to train dogs for hunting and hunt test competition. He marveled at the little dog's enthusiasm for retrieving a duck wing. We discussed the extent of the dog's problems, and that the surgical cost to remedy her conditions would be very high. After hundreds of puppy kisses and more remarkable retrieving exhibitions, the man reluctantly decided to take his deposit back and look for a different puppy.

As his truck turned out of the driveway, the puppy, who I had named Little Maggie, sat on the front porch of our farm house with me and her mother Clancy Girl. Maggie snuggled into my lap and as our eyes locked, she seemed to be asking, "Since no one else wants me and I'm the leftover, can I stay here with you and Clancy?"

The first of Maggie's five surgeries relieved the pain caused by her lower canines pushing into her palate. For three months, her mouth was wired with splints and spacers, but her attitude and spirit always said, "Thank you for keeping me alive—let's have some fun."

The correction of the entropic eye took two surgeries and a specialist at the University of Wisconsin Veterinary School. Maggie was seven months old, and she had a tremendous desire to retrieve, and to please me—the leader of her pack. Even during the six weeks she wore a protective surgical cone on her head, her spirit and enthusiasm remained strong. Occasionally, while racing to retrieve a training dummy, the lower lip of the plastic cone would dig into the earth, flipping Maggie into an awkward somersault. The cone made retrieving trickier, but Maggie was accustomed to difficulties, and she always figured out a way to get the job done.

Maggie's first real hunt happened when she was eighteen months old. We were hunting on the Mississippi River with a dog-training friend. The only chance for Maggie to retrieve a duck that morning came when our friend reported that he and his dog were unable to find a hen mallard he had knocked down in a thick patch of lily pads. We decided to let our dogs make one last attempt to find the duck. After a short hunt, Maggie swam to a nearby island, put her nose to the ground, and disappeared into the thick cover. After fifteen minutes, convinced she was either lost or hurt, I was relieved to see Maggie swimming back to the boat with a very lively hen mallard in her mouth. Maggie was indeed becoming a very special dog.

Maggie used her hunting instincts, and a little of my training to help her recover the duck. My dog-training techniques are more about being fair and respecting the animal, and are less about loud yelling and intimidation. Dogs sense if we like them or not, and it's in their nature to please the boss. Reassuring a dog with praise and encouragement builds the confidence and enthusiasm retrievers need to be strong hunters, and to make progress in their training for hunt test competition.

HRCH Cedar Ponds Little Maggie MH was titled Hunting Retriever Champion at the age of three, and AKC Master Hunter at four. She loves to hunt, run hunt tests, lie next to the wood stove, and sleep on my bed. Everything in her life is done with the same determined enthusiasm that kept her alive as a puppy.

Maggie has taught me much about giving and receiving love, and living in the moment. Her life embodies the truth that although life is often difficult, with the right attitude, life is also joy and happiness. Nobody else wanted the runt dog with a bad eye and deformed jaw, and Clancy and I are glad they didn't. Maggie has become a special dog in our pack. And all she needed was a chance to live, some ducks to retrieve, and lots of love.

GRANDFATHER GEORGE

Grandfather George was kneeling in the
moonlight next to the dead deer….
His long silver hair spilled over the shoulders
of his brown-and-red woolen shirt.

As she and her dog turned and walked away, sunlight reflected off her long jet-black pony tail. Her movement was mesmerizing, her beauty and grace overwhelming.

Stephanie and her dog Max had just competed in a field trial against me and my dog Cody Ann. That evening, staring at her business card, I remembered her clear green eyes that had looked directly into mine, and how her high sculpted cheek bones and smooth, olive-colored skin framed the beauty of her wide smile. I needed to know more about this woman. So I decided to make the call.

The moment I heard her voice on the phone, my mind went blank.

"Ugh, how's Max, and you?" I mumbled.

"We're ok, but we'd be a lot better if you and Cody hadn't beat us up so badly in the afternoon series."

"Better luck next time, Stephanie. So how about dinner Saturday night?"

During our first date at a small and romantic restaurant, I learned that Stephanie's Anglo father was an attorney who had disappeared many years ago. Her mother, a Lakota Sioux Indian, had grown-up on the Pine Ridge Reservation in South Dakota. When they were young, her mother had taken Stephanie and her siblings to Pine Ridge every summer to spend time with family. The Lakota community loved children, and taught them how to ride horses, make dream catchers, tell stories, and shoot bow and arrow.

Stephanie also spoke lovingly of her aged grandfather who lived on the reservation. Grandfather George had built his home by hand from stones, logs, hides, and mud—all gifts from the Earth Mother. It was a small home, but to him it was a sacred place. George sold herbal medicines that he gathered on the reservation, and bows and arrows that he made in his home.

One of Stephanie's most vivid memories was of shooting George's bows and arrows with her brothers. Once, her younger brother killed a jackrabbit with an arrow, and proudly ran to show George the dead animal. Stephanie remembered how their grandfather had taken the rabbit gently in his hands. Laying it next to his fire pit, he walked around the circular hearth with outstretched arms while quietly chanting a Lakota prayer. Then Grandfather George turned toward his grandson.

"So, how are you going to use the sacred body of brother rabbit?"

Carrots, wild turnips, and rabbit meat made the stew for that evening's meal.

■ ■ ■

Two months after our dinner date, Stephanie called to tell me that in three weeks, a cousin was coming from Pine Ridge for a visit, and that he was bringing Grandfather George along. She asked if it was possible for me to take her grandfather bow hunting for deer on my farm. The prospect of hunting with a Lakota Elder who still retained many of the traditional ways of the Plains Indians was indeed exciting.

"Of course," I replied. "I'd love to hunt with your Grandfather George."

During the next few weeks, I scouted for deer sign, and placed tree stands in locations that would provide good bow shots of fifteen yards or less. I trimmed out shooting lanes and erected wooden ladders, fastening them to the trees to make it easier for the old man to get up onto the shooting platforms.

The night they arrived, I sat down to dinner with Stephanie, her cousin, and her grandfather. Once Stephanie made the introductions, I immediately started talking about bow hunting in Wisconsin, and how the bucks were really getting into their rutting activities.

The old man smiled, listened politely, and replied, "I have a gift for you."

Reaching into the pocket of his faded red flannel shirt, he handed me an archery shooting glove that he had made from the hide of an antelope.

"This glove will make your arrows fly straight and true."

"Thank you, Grandfather. Most bow hunters use mechanical trigger releases, and they've never even seen a shooting glove."

George said nothing, and just continued to smile.

That evening over dinner, we talked about family, and how difficult life on the reservation had become. I listened as George spoke of poverty, crime, alcoholism, and drug addiction. Ancient traditions and rituals were disappearing as elders died, and very few of the younger generation were interested in keeping the Native traditions and language alive.

I asked George how hunting was on the reservation, and his two-word answer was, "Very poor."

The conversation shifted to bow hunting in Wisconsin. I assured Grandfather George that he would likely see some "good bucks" over the weekend. The old man shifted uncomfortably in his chair, and the quizzical expression on his face seemed to be silently asking, "What is a not-good buck?" When it came to hunting and killing animals, it was becoming clear that George and I spoke very different languages.

During the drive to my farm, George recalled his boyhood, and how members of his band had bow hunted for whitetail and mule deer in South

Dakota. "Walkers" would move with the wind through the dense vegetation of river and stream beds, driving the deer slowly toward "shooters" hiding near the animals' likely escape routes.

Out of respect for the animal, running shots were never taken as they risked inflicting a nonlethal wound. If a deer was killed, George explained that the hunters always released the deer's spirit, and spoke words of gratitude to the Earth Mother for the life-giving energy the meat would provide for the people.

At the farm, before heading to the woods, George took two practice shots at a Styrofoam deer target that was leaning against my barn. Both of his shots were from ten yards, and he hit the target perfectly on both tries.

George had made his bow out of a small ash tree that had grown close to his home. The bow was about fifty inches long. The handle was covered with a soft piece of brain-tanned antelope hide. He rested the arrow in the "V" formed by the bow and the knuckle of his right index finger, and drew the bow by pinching the gut-and-sinew string between his left thumb and the second knuckle of his index finger.

My plan was to have George hunt from a tree stand that would put his scent over Cedar Lake, and provide a good close shot at deer coming to feed in a nearby clover and alfalfa field.

As we approached the stand, George said, "I'll hunt along the edge of the oak woods next to the cattails."

I was disappointed that after all my effort, the old man decided not to hunt from the tree stand, but rather to strike out on his own and hunt on the ground.

"I'll meet you at the house after dark," George said, as he silently disappeared into the woods.

I wondered if the old man could find his way back to the house in the dark, or if he even had a flashlight.

■ ■ ■

The sun disappeared below the horizon as the night chill began to arrive. It was well past legal hunting hours as I walked in the moonlight toward the house. I worried about the old man; he might be injured or lost in the woods. What would Stephanie think if her grandfather got lost or hurt while hunting with me?

I turned toward the hardwoods, angry with myself for letting him go off alone, straining to hear a shout or see a light in the cold darkness. Just as I opened my mouth to yell for George, I became aware of a still presence in the darkness.

"I've been waiting for you," the old man said in a hushed voice.

"It's late, where have you been?"

"I killed a deer this evening" he whispered, handing me a bloody wooden arrow.

"I was worried you were lost, or hurt. Tell me what happened—tell me about the deer!"

George lowered himself into a squat and rested his tired back against the trunk of a small chokecherry tree.

"Brother Hawk hunts well from a tree, but my bones are old and the earth is soft and welcoming to my moccasins, so I decided to let you have the tree stand. In the hardwoods, there's a good escape trail that angles out of the cattails and passes close to a blown-down cedar tree. A buck and two does ran out of the cattails after you got into the tree stand, and they stopped close—maybe ten yards from the windfall I was hiding in."

"Was he a good buck?" I interrupted.

"His horns were pure white, like ivory, but I had my eye on the big doe. She was fat and stood at a perfect angle for a good killing shot."

"The horns—they were white and high?" I gestured. "And wide?"

The old Indian nodded his head, and slowly stood up.

"My God! You had Old White Horns at ten yards and you shot the doe? I've been hunting him for three years! He must be a typical 160-class or better Pope and Young record-book buck. White Horns at ten yards," I muttered incredulously, dropping the bloody arrow in disgust. "I just can't believe this."

George stared silently at the almost-full moon rising in the eastern sky.

"I'll meet you at the house later," the old man said solemnly. "I have some thanks to make and some work to do."

George picked up the broken arrow and slid it carefully into his fringed leather back quiver. Without another word, the old Indian quietly slipped into the moonlit woods.

I started for the house to feed the dogs and call Stephanie, when an owl hooted from a nearby tree, stopping me in my tracks. Immediately, another owl answered from the hardwoods, just about where George said he had killed the deer. Suddenly, I was filled with remorse for chastising Grandfather George for shooting the doe instead of the record-book buck. The owl in the hardwoods called again, and I knew that this was a sacred moment, and that I needed to be with George to share the experience with him.

I hung my bow, quiver, and pack in a box elder tree and crashed blindly through the dogwood and cattails. When I found him, George was kneeling in the moonlight next to the dead deer. His face and hands were raised toward the western sky.

"George, I'm so sorry for being such a jerk back there," I pleaded. "Please, let me help you with your deer."

The old man did not acknowledge my clumsy and noisy arrival. His eyes remained closed, and his long silver hair spilled over the shoulders of his faded brown-and-red woolen shirt. I sat silently at the base of the fallen cedar tree, embarrassed, reeling with emotion and feeling very small. I watched as the Lakota Elder gave thanks and honored the Spirit of the deer.

"O, sacred power of the place where the sun goes down, this day is *Wakan* [sacred]. The spirit of this deer has been released today."

Still kneeling and moving sun-wise, to the north, Grandfather George chanted, "O, Thunder-being, where Waziah has his lodge, who comes with purifying winds on wings that never tire, take the spirit of this four-legged, a gift from the Earth Mother."

Facing toward the eastern sky, the old Lakota cried, "O, sacred being of the place where the sun rises, who controls knowledge and brings light to the world, let us know the bounty of Mother Earth, and learn to be generous with the body of the deer, and help those in need with the meat of this four-legged."

Moving to the south he asked, "O, sacred being who controls all life in the universe, may this four-legged's Spirit have a good journey, and may this Spirit help us walk the sacred path in a manner pleasing to Wakan Tanka."

When I looked up, Grandfather George was standing next to the body of the deer. He tossed an offering of tobacco to the west, the north, the east, the south, to the earth, and finally to the sky.

Nothing moved in the quiet woods until George said, "Come. Help me skin the deer. Her meat will be cool and sweet for our breakfast in the morning."

Back at the house, my two yellow Labradors greeted us excitedly with food bowls in their mouths.

While the dogs ate a late dinner, I looked into the old man's dark eyes and said, "George, I..."

But Grandfather George held up his right hand and simply said, "I know. We are of different ways—the old and the new. Thank you for helping me skin our deer, and I'm glad to know that White Horns still waits in your dreams."

That night we ate fried deer heart and onions. I didn't tell George stories about the three Pope and Young bucks mounted on the wall of my living room, and he didn't ask any questions about them. Instead, we talked about the old ways—sweat lodges, sun dances, sacred pipes, and gentleness—the medicine of the deer.

Lakota storytellers like George say that deer teach us to use the power of gentleness to touch the hearts and minds of wounded beings. The ancient stories use the deer to illustrate gentleness—like the beginnings of a summer breeze. They teach us to stop pushing so hard to get others to change, and to love them as they are. The medicine of the deer teaches that if we do these things gently, we will connect with the Earth Mother, and the Great Spirit will guide us to peace.

Since my time with Grandfather George, a knowingness has grown within me that I am connected at the depth of my soul to something much greater than myself and the material world. The earth and sky are welcoming friends to me now, and I believe they should be protected for fellow and future travelers. Hunting is no longer the commercialized game it once was for me. Now it's a personal, spiritual, and emotional experience that recognizes and honors the sacredness of an animal's life.

The pace of my life has slowed as well. My new way of being is to try to be more like George—respecting the old ways and honoring Mother Earth.

I think of George when I read Sigurd Olson, who wrote, "When one finally arrives at the point where schedules are forgotten, and becomes immersed in ancient rhythms, one begins to live."

George has become an ancient rhythm in my bones and in my life.

After losing her job at a small bank that failed with the collapse of Wall Street, Stephanie reluctantly left Wisconsin and returned to her roots on the Pine Ridge Reservation. With the passing of time, our correspondence diminished and eventually ended.

Years later, while sorting through a stack of Christmas cards that had arrived in the mail, my heart skipped as I stared at a light blue envelope with a Pine Ridge, South Dakota return address. My hands trembled as I opened the envelope and read Stephanie's greeting:

> *Hello Howard:*
> *Merry Christmas and I hope you are happy and at peace. Grandfather George died this year during a sweat lodge ceremony. He was 94 years old, growing spiritually, still living mostly in the old ways, but with some of the new. He often told the story of hunting with you, and of the doe he shot on your farm. He always wondered if you ever met up again with White Horns. Before he died, he asked that I give you thanks for showing him some of the new ways and that he hoped your life was in alignment with your Spirit.*
> *Grandfather George had a good heart, and so do you.*
> *Your Friend,*
> *Stephanie*

GLAD TO BE HERE

It is not what you look at that matters, it's what you see.

—*Henry David Thoreau*

Robert Peterson was a very happy man. He had caught and released over a dozen fat and beautiful Yellowstone Cutthroat trout. The soothing sound of Montana's Lamar River reminded him of how grateful he was to be alive and free.

Closing his eyes, Robert said out loud, "Thank you, Great Spirit, for these incredible blessings."

A loud grunt jolted Robert out of his peaceful meditative state. On the opposite bank of the river, a mere thirty yards away, stood an enormous male bison staring at him with shiny black eyes. Robert stared back, in awe of the beast's large and muscular anatomy. A moment later, the buffalo—*tatanka* to the Plains Indians—switched his short tail and slowly returned to the herd that was grazing in the valley.

Relieved, Robert lay back into the coolness of the grass and watched the gathering cumulus clouds move across the big Montana sky. As one cloud overtook and merged into another, Robert visualized a young Lakota hunter riding bareback on a spirited pony, chasing stampeding *tatanka* across the Great Plains.

Robert imagined the young hunter drawing his powerful bow and sinking an obsidian-tipped arrow deep into the chest of a large male bison. Foamy blood poured from its lungs as the *tatanka* weakened and slowed just long enough for the Indian to drive a second lethal shaft into the bull's ribs. The great beast staggered and collapsed onto the prairie, gasping for air.

The young Indian jumped from his pony and gave thanks to the Great Spirit, Wakan Tanka, for the life and body of the animal that would sustain his family.

The air began to calm and Robert was grateful that his imagination had allowed him to be part of the drama of the buffalo hunt in the clouds. The sun was rapidly disappearing behind the mountains that stood sentinel on the western flank of the river valley. It was past time to head back to his truck, but for some reason, Robert felt compelled to stay, to wait, and to let the approaching darkness surround and engulf him.

The chill of the approaching night reminded him of historical accounts of white hunters killing millions of bison and taking only their hides and their tongues. Hundreds of millions of pounds of life-sustaining meat lay in stinking, rotting piles of death and decay on America's Great Plains, while locomotives hauled the hides to Eastern tanneries. The descriptions of huge piles of sun-bleached bones, and the near extermination of the great bison herds, left Robert feeling a dark and heavy shame for the foul practices and mentality of the white "hide-men."

The nearly full moon poked its luminous face above the rim of the mountains. Robert's memory drifted back to another time in his own life, many years before. His young life had been filled with excitement and hope, and the love of a woman. They had been establishing the foundations of a future together. He had believed that she would sustain him throughout his life. The soft, billowing clouds he had watched that afternoon reminded him of her delicate beauty and gentleness.

But as the moon lit up the broad night sky, Robert's mood changed. The dark night of the soul had come to Robert's life, one night long ago. He remembered with a chill the loud ringing of his telephone, and the haunting words of a sobbing woman on the on line.

"Do you know what your girlfriend has been doing with my husband?" the voice asked.

Standing in the kitchen of the farmhouse they had recently purchased, Robert weakly whispered, "No. Please tell me."

He was sickened by her answer.

He finally had managed to stammer, "Thank you for calling. I'm so sorry for this awful hurt. Goodbye."

Robert felt gutted and discarded, like the rotting buffalo carcasses on the prairie.

■ ■ ■

Robert's breathing became labored as he relived that night in his mind's eye. He had sat there in stunned silence, rocking in the chair they had recently purchased at a garage sale for their new home. The joints of the wooden chair squeaked rhythmically, and Casey, their yellow Labrador dog, watched and listened as the chair's monotonous song wore on into the early morning hours.

There had been no sleep for Robert. Instead, there were tears of sadness, a tightening anger in his gut, and a deep-seated sense of bewilderment.

"What have I done?" he asked Casey, as the dog cautiously inched closer to the chair. "I should have known that the late hours at the office had nothing to do with business," he sighed, as he buried his face in his trembling hands.

At 8:20 a.m. on that dark Sunday morning, Robert heard her car pull into the driveway. The car door slammed. Moments later, she came into the kitchen.

"You're up awfully early for a Sunday morning."

"Where have you been all night? Why didn't you call?" he had demanded.

"I stayed at Jane's house. We played Scrabble. I drank too much wine to drive home, and I didn't want to wake you with a phone call."

■ ■ ■

Robert Peterson sat on a flat stone and rested his back against the bank of the Lamar River. Montana's big sky glittered with constellations, and an occasional meteor glowed brightly, faded, and disappeared.

Although he desperately tried to keep his thoughts in the present, Robert's mind kept being drawn back to that unbearable time in his life when he felt so hopeless and lonely. Although he had pleaded and negotiated with her, one day she gathered her belongings and left for a new life with the other man.

Robert's grief was enormous, and he tried desperately to forget, and to numb the pain. His drinking increased dramatically, and Robert met women in bars who seemed as lonely and desperate as he was.

He talked with his close friends about his despair in the wake of the abrupt ending of his eleven-year relationship. They had offered, "It wasn't like you were married." Or, "There are plenty of fish in the sea; just go find another."

Robert was startled out of his dreamlike state by the thwack of a beaver's tail hitting the polished black surface of the Lamar River. The luminous face of his digital watch revealed that it was almost 10:00 p.m., and he thought about Cody Ann, his beautiful five-year-old yellow Lab who had been locked in the back of his pickup truck since noon. He knew that no matter how neglectful he had been, Cody would wiggle excitedly and wag her tail in delight upon his return.

A peaceful smile crept across his face as he recalled the companionship and love he had shared with his dogs, Sam, Casey, Clancy Girl, Little Maggie, and now Cody Ann.

Casey was the dog that had comforted Robert the night he had rocked in the chair, waiting, and sick with worry about his future. And Casey was the dog who had moved close to his chair, looking at Robert with knowing, gentle, and loving brown eyes. Casey was the dog that watched intently as Robert had solemnly removed the Remington 12-gauge shotgun from the walnut gun cabinet and loaded it with one deadly red shell.

Casey had danced with joy, believing that Robert was finally taking her hunting again. But something was dreadfully wrong. Casey followed at a distance with lowered ears as Robert slowly climbed the carpeted stairs to the second floor of the farmhouse in which his now-dying dreams had been built.

Robert Peterson's thoughts were not about hunting ducks or pheasants, but rather how dark and unbearably dismal his life had become. There had been no light or joy in his life for a long time. There were only sickening hangovers, despair, and more failed attempts to replace the love which, fourteen months prior, had walked out of his life forever. He could not think of one reason why he should continue to endure such pain.

The smooth black steel of the gun lay cold in his shaking hands as he checked the chambered shell and the trigger safety mechanism one last time. Robert Peterson had peacefully closed his eyes and was preparing to end his life, when he felt Casey's cold and wet nose on the left side of his neck and cheek. Gently, she laid her broad Labrador head on his left shoulder, and he could feel her warm exhales on his ear and face.

Robert set the gun down and placed his hand on her soft, still head.

"It's okay, girl," he whispered.

She pushed closer to Robert and thumped the floor tentatively with her powerful tail. Robert's eyes welled with tears as he lay down on the floor with Casey in his embrace, and convulsively sobbed away his deadly thoughts. The dog gently licked his salty, tear-stained face, and Robert's pain was overtaken by the depth of the connection and love he and Casey felt for each other.

"You're the reason I'll stay alive today," he told her. "If I were gone, who'd take you hunting? And another owner might be mean to you. We need each other, Casey. Thank you for being here."

Robert Peterson and his loving friend Casey descended the stairs together and walked into the sunlight of the beautiful world. They drove to a nearby lake and he threw bumpers, which Casey eagerly retrieved until they were both happily exhausted.

■ ■ ■

The moon seemed to brighten as it climbed ever higher into the night sky. The flat stone that he was resting on suddenly felt hard and uncomfortable.

Robert shifted and stood up to stretch his cramped legs and stiff lower back, and at that moment, grace revisited his rested psyche. After thirty-one years, he suddenly knew with perfect clarity that the love he had experienced in that special connection with another human being was still alive in his heart. That evening, there on the banks of the Lamar River, he knew that the ache and hurt of that tortured part of his history was gone forever. Compassion and love and forgiveness rushed into his being to take their place.

For years, Robert had nurtured the anger and hurt that had resulted from that betrayal. He had tried to navigate the treacherous waters of new relationships and had failed.

One woman had sadly remarked to Robert, "You have a sentry that tirelessly patrols the perimeter of your heart."

And she had been correct. Robert had been living in the limitations of hurt, and not in the life-giving nurturance of love and forgiveness.

That night on the Lamar River, Robert suddenly knew that in order for love to grow and do its healing work, it must be given and received with compassion and without conditions. This must have been the purpose which he had survived to fulfill! To live in the love that had been so generously bestowed upon him, and to give it back with equal generosity. That was how Robert would make life and the world more beautiful and enriching. He would bring forth the kindness, gentleness, and compassion of the love that still resided within his heart.

Yes. It was time.

■ ■ ■

Robert could barely discern the dark outlines of the buffalo that lay in the grassy field on the opposite side of the river. He thought about the eyes of the large bull that had stared into his eyes earlier that day—eyes of a species very nearly extinct—locking with the eyes of a man who had walked the rim of that same black abyss of extinction.

Again, the powerful rush of connection and clear understanding flowed through Robert, as he gazed at the bison resting peacefully beneath the night sky. Recalling a poem written by Rumi, the thirteenth-century Sufi poet, he recited the ancient words for the benefit of the *tatanka*, for the river, for himself, and for all of the life in the valley:

> *Out beyond the ideas of wrong-doing and right-doing, there is a field.*
> *I will meet you there.*
> *When the soul lies down in that grass, the world is too full to talk about.*

Robert Peterson lay back down in the grass and was silent.

■ ■ ■

It was very late, but the moon brightened the path through the willows and sage that led back to his truck. Cody Ann was sleeping soundly on an orange carpet remnant. As Robert searched and fumbled for the keys hidden under the back bumper, Cody scrambled to her feet. Her thick Labrador tail banged excitedly against the inside wall of the fiberglass topper, and she whined impatiently as he twisted the handle to open the rear window.

"I'm glad we're here," Robert said. "I love you, Cody."

She licked his face and wiggled with enthusiasm, happy as he was to be reconnected.

Robert sat on the truck's tailgate, sipping coffee that had lost most of its heat during the past twelve hours. He watched Cody's smooth lines and graceful movement as she hunted for scent in the sage brush. Glancing back into the Lamar River Valley, he could no longer see the *tatanka* lying in the grass, but he knew that they were there, and he was grateful and happy that he was here as well.

"Just look at this place," he yelled to Cody with wonder and disbelief in his voice. "Come on girl, it's time to go home."

■ ■ ■

It was well past midnight when Robert Peterson and Cody Ann drove through the wild blackness of Yellowstone Park's backcountry. Cody's head lay peacefully on Robert's lap, and his right hand reflexively stroked the softness of her ears and neck.

As Cody slept, Robert found himself humming Tim McGraw's, "Live Like You Were Dying,'"' a song about how a middle-aged man lived his life after being diagnosed with an incurable disease:

> *I went sky diving, I went rocky mountain climbing,*
> *I went two point seven seconds on a bull named Fu Man Chu.*
> *And I loved deeper and I spoke sweeter,*
> *And I gave forgiveness I'd been denying.*

Robert Peterson knew how he was going to live the rest of his precious life. And he was filled with gratitude that he was still alive to start that journey, with less fear and more love in his heart. Welcome home.

TROUT FRIENDS

You knew what you had to do...
as you strode deeper and deeper
into the world,
determined to do
the only thing you could do—
determined to save
the only life you could save.

—Mary Oliver, "The Journey"

Robert Peterson was drawn to the adventure and mystery of the American West. He longed to explore Montana's pristine rivers, and its native trout and wild animals. This was his time, his truth, and his Spirit calling—and nobody could answer that call except Robert Peterson.

Throughout his life, there had been people who had pressured and persuaded him not to follow his heart—to say no to the calling of his inner voices. These external voices were loud and convincing: Stay home. And when your work for others is finished, then you may pursue your dreams.

But this was his time, and Robert Peterson finally turned to the calling of his True Self and said, *Yes, I will follow you.*

Robert's crew on his expedition were his two yellow Labs, Clancy Girl and her daughter Little Maggie. Fly rods, waders, a kayak, a mountain tent, and a book of maps were loaded into his pickup truck—the dogs, of course, sat up front with Robert. As he pulled out of the driveway, Robert knew in his heart that he had made the right choice—he was free of the voices shouting their bad advice. He was on an adventure and journey to *do the only thing [he] could do, to save the only life [he] could save.*

The dogs quickly fell asleep in the back seat, and Robert smiled from a place deep within himself, a place that had been asleep for years. His Spirit was awakening, his heart was in sunlight, and the highway west said "Welcome."

■ ■ ■

Robert was fascinated with the journal descriptions of the wildness of western America, and the harrowing experiences the men on the 1804 Lewis and Clark expedition had endured. He wondered if he could have survived the perils of hostile Indians, capsized canoes, and freezing rain. Those same dangers had bonded the men of the expedition into a highly functioning team of friends who depended upon each other, and who ultimately survived in a beautiful but often savage new world. The journals also reveal that many of the men, including the two leaders, remained friends for many years after the Corps of Discovery returned home.

While traveling through the Missouri River drainage in North Dakota, Robert stopped often to paddle out into the river to view the locations that are colorfully described in Lewis and Clark's journals. Except for a few houses and convenience stores, many of the places described by the explorers look about the same as they did over 200 years ago.

Lewis brought Seaman, his Newfoundland dog, along on the expedition. The dog slept in the keelboat, rode the rivers and rapids in their canoes, and ate elk meat while sitting around campfires with the men. Like Seaman, Clancy and Maggie accompanied Robert as he paddled along the banks of the Missouri and swam in the river's swift, cold water.

After traveling all night, Robert and his dogs finally arrived at the Big Horn River in southeastern Montana. Although he had never fished trout west of the Mississippi, Robert climbed into his kayak and started fishing.

By midmorning, Robert was casting a small white dry fly to trout on the Big Horn. He had no idea what the trout were feeding on, or even the name of the fly that he was clumsily casting. Although other fishermen seemed to be hooking and landing a considerable number of trout, Robert had only succeeded in snagging one large brown trout that broke his leader and diminished his hope of landing a Big Horn trout.

"How's it goin'?" came the friendly inquiry from a slightly balding man in a passing drift boat.

"Haven't landed one yet, but I'm going to try a new fly."

"My name is Earl. Mind if I pull in below you and try some PMD emergers on these guys?"

Earl's approach reminded Robert of ice fishing back home in Wisconsin, where overbearing fishermen would encroach on his fishing spot by drilling holes in the ice within six feet of where he was catching fish.

Earl kept smiling while angling his drift boat toward Robert's kayak that was beached on a nearby sandbar.

"Sure, come on. Maybe I can learn something about fishing trout," Robert said, waving his right arm in a semi-welcoming gesture.

Earl James was about ten years younger than Robert. He had a quick and contagious laugh and a swollen lower lip that appeared to be filled with tobacco. His arms and legs were deeply tanned, and the worn treads of his expensive wading sandals indicated that he had earned many stream-miles of trout-fishing experience.

"Let's take a look at your leader," he smiled, clipping off Robert's ragged, knot-filled monofilament tippet. "I'm from Houston," Earl reported, as he tied a new nine-foot tapered leader onto Robert's fly line.

Earl patiently explained that PMD abbreviates Pale Morning Dun, a small yellowish mayfly that trout love to eat.

"Ok. So what's an emerger?" Robert asked hesitantly.

Earl gave a brief explanation of the life cycle of the insect. Then he and Robert took turns casting to the trout that continued to feed hungrily on the PMDs. Robert hooked the first fish on his third cast. The sixteen-inch rainbow trout leapt out of the water as it charged toward the opposite side of the river. With gentle and reassuring coaching about rod position and reeling in slack line, Earl skillfully netted Robert's first Montana trout.

"You gotta take my picture. The guys back home won't believe this!"

With the video camera running, Earl complimented and congratulated Robert on his trout, and the two high-fived and backslapped their way back to the bend in the river where trout continued to gorge themselves. After two hours and many more pictures of fifteen-to-twenty-inch brown and rainbow trout, Earl invited Robert to tie his kayak to the back of Earl's drift boat so they could fish together for the rest of the day.

■ ■ ■

That afternoon on Montana's legendary Big Horn River, Earl James and Robert Peterson connected and became trout friends. Trout friends bond by netting big trout for each other; taking the trusted friend to a "secret spot" without worrying that it will be disclosed to anyone else; giving a trout friend a fly that's catching fish when no other fly is working; and after a night of fishing, getting lost in the woods together while trying to find their way back to the truck.

As long as there is a cold and clean river with hope of hooking a fish, trout friends can plan their lives so that they will be able to meet at their secret and sacred fishing spots for years to come.

That special day in August, Earl James and Robert Peterson laughed in the sunlight bouncing off the Big Horn's dancing water and told stories about their lives. While casting a Henryville caddis to rising trout, Earl talked openly about having just sold the business he had lovingly built in order to settle an emotionally painful and confusing divorce. While Earl fished and shared secrets and feelings from his heart, Robert rowed the drift boat to the best of his ability, avoiding at least some of the moss-covered boulders that litter the bottom of the Big Horn.

When Earl rowed, Robert fished from the bow of the drift boat and spoke honestly about the most recent casualty in his history of failed relationships. The caddis kept hatching, and Robert kept talking and casting, catching a few trout, and occasionally snagging Earl's T-shirt or the anchor rope.

Two fishermen meeting by chance in the wondrous natural environment of a trout river, sharing deep feelings, swapping knowledge and fishing techniques, netting each other's fish, rowing skillfully so that the other gets a good cast angle on a rising trout—all these things bond them into a team. They become trout friends.

As the fishing slowed, Earl and Robert drifted in silence down the river. They watched otters as they played on a gravel bar. They spotted a muskrat chewing on cattails and a beaver swimming upstream with a freshly cut alder branch in its mouth. Eagles and osprey fished along with the trout friends as they floated through the unspeakable beauty of the Big Horn River canyon.

In the midst of the birds and fish and animals, and a river overflowing with life-giving energy, Earl and Robert had talked of life's pains and disappointments. But they also talked about hope and the excitement and anticipation of saying yes to life, and of saying yes to the voices from within that beckon one to follow his own journey.

In the failing evening light, the boat landing and parking area finally materialized. Robert wondered out loud if Lewis and Clark and their men had been appreciative and thrilled to be in this place, and if they too had become trout friends.

Clancy and Maggie wagged their thick Labrador tails in enthusiastic hellos and plunged into the river. Earl loaded his boat onto the trailer, while Robert tied the kayak onto its carrying rack. The new trout friends decided to camp together, and they floated and fished and talked and laughed on the Big Horn River for a few more days before saying, "Goodbye for now, and good fishing."

■ ■ ■

During the last weeks of August, Earl fished and explored the Madison and Gallatin rivers near West Yellowstone, Montana, and Robert fished

Rock Creek and other streams in Idaho's Bitterroot Mountains. Every few days, Robert would call Earl with excited reports about PMD and Blue Wing Olive hatches—and one day about catching an eighteen-inch brown trout on an imitation flying ant. Now and then, Earl would call and tell Robert about the community and culture of trout-fishing guides that exists in the Madison River Valley. He was becoming trout friends with some of the guides, and he was particularly anxious for Robert to meet a guy named Chris, who guided for Bud Lilly's Trout Shop in West Yellowstone.

■ ■ ■

On the trip home, Robert stopped to fish a few of the "secret" places that he and Earl had discovered on the Big Horn River. Clancy and Maggie chased each other in a shallow backwater as Robert slipped into a quiet and reflective place in his now-calmed and healing psyche. Robert's journey west had been less about escaping and more about discovering long-ignored truths about himself. The rivers and mountains, the sky and his new trout friend Earl, all had helped Robert untether himself from a materialistic world which demanded more than he could deliver. For years, he had been saying yes to the wrong voices for the wrong reasons. Finally, he had said yes to the unlived life that summoned him.

Perhaps for the first time in his life, Robert experienced the sensations of completion, contentment, and serenity. The day was ending, and the road home was long, so he reluctantly whistled for the dogs to load up. Exhausted, Clancy and Maggie were falling asleep on the back seat as the truck turned onto the eastbound highway. Robert felt that smile coming again from deep down in his soul. He had connected with his dogs, his Spirit, and a new trout friend. Life wasn't so crazy anymore, and it felt good to be going home.

BROTHER HAWK

When we are no longer able to change a situation,
we are challenged to change ourselves.

—*Victor E. Frankl*

My friend Jack is a Florida cracker, and he's proud of it. He hates, among other things, political correctness, fancy cars, Yankees (except for me), cops, tourists, and most minorities. And, he reserves for government regulators of commercial fishing—his lifelong occupation—a special place at the top of his lengthy enemies list.

I visited Jack one morning at his rural southwestern Florida homestead as he was replacing the ropes on his fishing nets and crab traps.

With hands on hips, and a slight grin, he snarled, "Oh my God, here comes that Yankee professor and his dog. If you'd showed up without Cody, I'd run your educated ass off my property and into the Gulf of Mexico!"

"Nice to see you as well, Jack. Get me some coffee with cream and I'll sit with you—as long as I can stand the company, and the insults."

Jack returned from his house with a round of coffees, and as we started back into our conversation, I was distracted by a large red-shouldered hawk perched on top of a nearby tree. Needing more rope for the net, Jack pulled on the black nylon rope that was lying in the deep grass. Instantly, the hawk dropped from his perch, and with predatory speed, he attacked the slow-moving rope with his deadly talons and powerful beak.

We were mesmerized.

"He thinks the rope's a snake," Jack whispered.

Realizing something was wrong, the hawk stepped back and cocked his head, then pounced again. Staring intently at the rope, the hawk mounted a desultory third attack, weakly grasping at the rope with one outstretched foot. Then, grudgingly accepting that the rope was not the snake he had believed it to be, and resigned to being powerless to change it into a tasty breakfast, the hawk flew back to his perch to continue his morning hunt and try to stay alive another day.

Looking up into the tree, Jack shook his head, saying, "Brother Hawk, you are such a dumb bird. How did you ever get this far in life?"

"The hawk is not dumb, Jack. He's our teacher today. How many times have you and I pounced on something or someone, who we believe is the solution to our problems and unhappiness in life?"

"Yah Professor, I know, you're talking about alcohol and my first ex-wife. She changed so much after we got married. And who wouldn't drink waking up next to a nag like her every morning?"

"Most of us believe there is one perfect person for us, somewhere out there—hiding in the grass. All we have to do is find them, and they'll magically do life's difficult work for us. It didn't happen with the last one; we must have made a mistake. So we try again."

Jack answered his cell phone, so I took a walk. I thought about how hopeful I felt with each new candidate, sure this one must be the perfect "other." But the illusion always fades, and hope eventually dies. The "other" is not magical, and they cannot do the self-actualizing work that we have unconsciously projected onto them. Indeed, the perfect and magical other person always turns out to be just another flawed and complicated human being.

Nothing—except maybe alcohol and drugs—seems to have more power over our perceptions and distortions of reality. Over and over, we return to our magical other, like the hawk returning to the rope, hoping they will change into the person we initially perceived them to be—our savior.

Eventually, the hope that he or she is the magical other will collapse. "Dammit, it's a rope, not a snake." "Oh, now I see, they're just another ordinary, wounded human being—not a God."

The other did not meet my projections. And, since I was not conscious or aware that I had made impossible projections onto the other, I can only blame them for deceiving me about who they really are. Our choices are to become aware of, and take responsibility for, our expectations of the other, or blame and resent them for the great disappointment of another unfulfilled dream.

Can we heal and try again? The hawk did, and it's almost guaranteed that we too will try again. But unless we become conscious of the unreality—indeed, the impossibility—of what we have been projecting onto the other, the outcome will be the same. We are responsible for our own truth and self-actualization—with the help and support of others who are willing to participate in our growth.

"Well, Mr. genius professor, how do we know, before we get married, if a woman is willing help us do these things?"

"Well, Mr. genius commercial fisherman—maybe we should ask them."

It was almost noon when Jack coiled the unused black nylon rope, and I finished my third cup of coffee. We agreed to meet that evening for dinner and continue our conversation about how to live happily by following one's own truth.

Turning out of Jack's yard, I thought about how difficult this planet is to live on, for humans, as well as for hawks. But since we have no other options, we must take the actions necessary to find the Spirit within us, and have the courage to live from that source of truth.

Wisdom of the ages tells us there are two compelling reasons for humans to be on a path leading toward finding their own authentic natures. First, that is how we will find love. And second, it is how we keep the ways of others from sweeping us, and our truths, away. Although tempted by instincts to follow the ways of others, we do so at the peril of following the wrong God, and missing our own star.

The path is long and often difficult, but only we—with the willing help of others—can do our own life's work. And it is already late enough; and so we begin—again.

BUD

The privilege of a lifetime is being who you are.

—Joseph Campbell

The old man's pipe glowed as he drew three short breaths, and then closed his mouth to think. I watched intently for wisps of escaping smoke, but only when he spoke again did faint signs of his exhale appear with each slow and measured word.

"You know, too damned many people told me how I ought to live my life, and I was dumb enough to listen. Now I'm running out of time to fix it."

The arthritic knuckles of his once-powerful right hand were easy to discern beneath his age-spotted skin. He inserted the pipe back into its familiar groove, and I heard a muffled click as the stem found its home between his stained and worn molars.

"Why didn't I go to Alaska when I was young and strong?" he asked, gazing into space. "First it was the kids, then it was a new job, then my hunting buddy had a heart attack, then the wife took ill, and now, I'm too old and can't walk."

While Bud was talking, my thoughts turned to the stories about hunting in Alaska that I had read in outdoor magazines.

My eyes locked with Bud's as I said out loud for the first time in my life, "I'm forty-two years old, and I've dreamed of bow hunting Alaska ever since I was twelve."

"Well then, dammit, go! Don't let this happen to you," he shouted, kicking angrily at his walker.

The next day, I dug out a Fred Bear video and called my one bow-hunting friend who had created enough freedom in his life to possibly say yes to an Alaskan adventure. We watched the video, and the deal was done. Don and I agreed on an August Alaskan bow-hunting trip for caribou, and possibly black bear. Cost of the trip and objections from other people didn't matter—we were going to Alaska!

I called Bud the next morning. His daughter answered the phone.

"He's still in bed, but awake enough to smoke his pipe," she said merrily, handing him the phone.

Excitedly, I told Bud I was going to Alaska in August and it was all because of our talk in his kitchen.

"You go, and have a great hunt. And bring me back a bear steak!"

For the first time in years, Bud sounded alive and excited—and so was I.

When the news of our plans leaked out, my mother worried about small aircraft crashing into mountains and grizzly bear attacks. My father asked bluntly how much the trip would cost. He winced and shook his head in silent disapproval when I told him a number approximately half of the actual figure.

Don's boss was incredulous that an employee of eighteen years would brazenly ask for two weeks off during their busy season. The vacation approval came slowly, and it was laced with guilt about letting down the team and disloyalty to the company.

The daunting mission of informing my girlfriend of five years of my Alaska plans caused me much distress. I finally settled on a strategy of delicately sprinkling my Alaska plans into the conversation during dinner at her favorite restaurant. The public venue and romantic atmosphere should soften her resistance.

The mood that evening seemed perfect.

I opened with, "It's been a lifelong dream of mine to bow hunt in Alaska, and I'm planning a trip for August."

"How long will you be gone?"

"Two weeks—at the most, but it may be less."

"You've never asked me to go on a two-week trip."

She set her silverware down and leaned back from the table. I was losing ground fast.

"Well, you pick the time and place, and we'll go there between now and August."

"I'll let you know. Let's leave. I'm finished," she said, standing stiffly.

My plan had failed miserably. There was no invitation to come in for coffee, or anything else. She said goodbye, and closed the door solidly on the passenger side of my pickup truck.

As she walked away, I softly uttered a plea:

"Bud, please help me not to be dumb enough to listen when others tell me how I ought to live my life."

Bud was with me that evening. I arrived home and joyfully hugged my two yellow Labradors that danced with delight when I opened the back door.

Standing in the darkness of my kitchen, I knew exactly how I was going to live my life. That night, it became clear that my soul and my heart would lead me to my truths and passions. And people like Bud would give me the courage and strength to say no to people who felt they had the right to control the direction and details of my life. Time is a gift, given to us one day at a time. Those who would take away my freedom of deciding how to use that precious gift must be told no.

August came, and Don and I flew into Anchorage, and then across the Cook Inlet to meet our bush pilot at a remote airstrip. We flew past vast glaciers, followed wild river channels, and passed over pristine lakes, caribou, mountain goats, and bear. The healing exhilaration that welled up from within us will remain in our bones forever. I wished that Bud could have been with us.

The bush pilot flew us over the tundra until we found suitable bow-hunting terrain with an abundance of caribou. On the first morning after fly-in, Don spotted the enormous antlers of a caribou as they passed through an opening in a strip of willow brush. After a short stalk, he killed the caribou with a perfect shot from his fifty-two-pound longbow and homemade wooden arrow. The excitement of the hunters was tempered by the deep respect we felt for the animal, and the beauty of the Alaskan wilderness.

On the second day, I decided to stalk a huge black bear that was feeding on blueberries.

"Are you absolutely sure this is a good idea?" Don asked.

I needed some encouragement, since stalking a bear of that caliber on the open tundra with a bow and arrow seemed like a crazy idea.

After playing the wind and terrain, I was finally presented with a thirty-five-yard quartering-away shot. The arrow hit about a foot behind the spot I had aimed at. The snarling bear bolted about thirty yards and stopped to bite at the wound. I launched a second arrow that hit dead center, heart and lungs. After smashing through a hundred yards of tag alders and willows, the bear was dead. He was lying on his back, staring at the sky with his left eye open, and a silvery scar where his right used to be.

Bud's Alaskan bear steaks were on the ground, but there was something wrong this time. Instead of jubilation after the kill, I felt a deep sadness in my heart for the bear. I thought about his history, as a newly born cub with his mother in their winter den, her lessons on how to survive in Alaska's wilderness, and summer days on the mountaintop lying comfortably in the sunshine with a full belly. And now this.

I talked with Don about how I was feeling, and he understood—he had experienced some of the same emotions. But there was skinning, quartering, and packing to be done, and a storm with high winds and cold rain was approaching from the west. So I buried my feelings and got to work. But, the recollection of that magnificent bear lying there lifeless, and of the shiny scar looking up at me, haunted me for many years.

During the flight home, I thought about the boxes of frozen caribou and bear meat that were in the plane's cargo hold. I remembered the second arrow, arching high over the tundra and disappearing into the bear's ribs—and the remorse I felt when we found him dead. And I thought about the companionship shared with a good friend in that wild place, and the gratitude I felt for Bud. That wise old man taught me the importance of following my passions and being who I am—no matter what other people might say.

After a few days of unpacking and rest, I called Bud to tell him that I had his bear steaks. His daughter answered and reported that Bud had been in the hospital for a week, and that I should visit him that day. When I walked into his room, some family members were there, and Bud was gasping for air from a respirator.

I sat with his daughter in the lounge for a few hours and showed her some pictures of the Alaskan trip. A nurse told us that visiting hours were almost over, so we stepped into Bud's room to say goodnight. He was breathing easily and seemed alert. When our eyes met, I gave him a thumbs-up and showed him a picture of the bear. A sly grin moved across his face, and when he winked at me, I knew that in some way, Bud had finally gotten to Alaska.

Bud died a few days later. I asked for his pipe, and his family has given it to me. I haven't smoked it yet, but while holding it in my hand, I noticed some age spots near my right thumb. The spots on my hands and the aches in my back don't concern me anymore because I've been to Alaska, and I'm going again next year—no matter what anybody says I ought to do.

Author's Note:
"Bud" is related to another story in this book: "Spirit Bear" is about my feeling of guilt over killing this one-eyed bear in Alaska, and how, after seventeen years, I was absolved by an act of forgiveness during a vision quest on the Big Horn River in Montana.

PART 3: LOST AND DISILLUSIONED

*Midway in life's journey I found myself in a
dark wood, having lost the way.*

—Dante, The Inferno

In midlife, the journey continues to be difficult. This is a time of reflection, reevaluation, and re-visioning. Many resist this inward turn, since it means that something needs to change; that something's gone wrong with the plan; that life is not fulfilling.

All of this was true in my life. Perhaps the trip felt crazy and wrong because I planned my life around other people's aspirations and beliefs instead of my own. And maybe the expectations I had about this journey were not realistic, since society's road map had led me nowhere—at least, nowhere that I wanted to be.

My view of how my life should fit into the world did not come from my heart and Spirit. Instead, it was dictated to me by family and culture. My mind raced in crazy directions. Confused and empty, I wondered why I felt so unfulfilled when outwardly, it appeared as if I was "living the dream."

In order to be restored to sanity, I had to find and connect with my own truth. This became my new life goal. And once again, my dogs led me back to the natural world—the place where I come alive, where I feel I belong.

The stories in this part are about people and experiences in nature, and the dogs that helped me answer the unavoidable question, "Who is the True Self that wants so desperately to live through me in this world?"

AWAKENING TO ONENESS AT HEBGEN LAKE, MONTANA

My purpose is to awaken to the illusion of my separateness.

—*Thich Nhat Hahn*

The life of a trout bum is good, Robert mused as he filleted the rainbow trout that he planned to eat for breakfast. He was a solid believer in the practice of catch-and-release, so it was unusual for him to kill and eat a trout. On that morning, however, his hunger for fish and the lack of alternative food allowed Robert Peterson to rationalize eating the beautiful Hebgen Lake trout.

The fish had been seduced by a dry fly that imitated a small mayfly called callibaetis. Robert had tied his favorite callibaetis fly that morning. The white calf-tail wings, pheasant quill body, and split tail all received the careful attention necessary to fool the cautiously selective trout of Hebgen Lake.

The callibaetis life cycle fascinated Robert, and he had spent many hours researching the entomology of the insect that is such an important link in the trout food chain. The cycle begins with a fertilized egg that grows into a nymph that emerges to the surface, then becomes an adult that mates and dies. The dead and dying flies float on the water and are gobbled-up by hungry trout. Very specific water temperature and precise water chemistry are necessary for the delicate and complex callibaetis to thrive and reproduce.

Prior to filleting the fish's flesh from its bony skeleton, Robert ceremoniously turned his face skyward, spread his arms wide, and repeated a prayer learned from a Native American friend:

> *Thank you, Wakan Tanka, for the gift of this fish. Its Spirit is sacred. Reveal to me the path that is yours, so that I may use the energy and strength from the flesh of the fish to live in a way that is pleasing to the Great Spirit.*

The surgically sharp blade of the wooden-handled knife slipped effortlessly through the trout's silver skin and firm pink flesh, settling on the cartilage and bone of its spine. The cutting edge then moved toward the trout's tail—the same powerful tail that over its lifetime had propelled the fish safely away from the deadly talons of osprey and eagles, and the hungry jaws of pelicans and otters. But on that morning, the same tail that had saved its life so many times in the past, had assisted the trout in catching a callibaetis imposter that concealed a sharp steel hook.

The knife's blade felt its way over the rib bones, and then moved swiftly out of the trout's body just ahead of its tail. Robert respectfully laid the carcass next to a rotting log, and silently prayed that insects, birds, and other forest creatures would share in the gift of the trout's body.

A pair of osprey displayed their aerobatic talents as they circled and soared into the azure Montana sky. They seemed to just be enjoying themselves by putting on a graceful show for anyone who cared to watch and share in the freedom of their lives.

Robert began to sense a connection to the trout, the sky, the osprey, and the earth. In that feeling and in that moment, there was no loneliness or seeking, and he had no desire to be anyplace but where he was. He was at peace.

■ ■ ■

Two pink fillets of rainbow trout, washed clean by the cold water of Hebgen Lake lay glistening on the truck's tailgate. As he began assembling his propane stove, Robert was startled by the simple realization that the trout's flesh was soon to become part of his own flesh.

Gazing out onto the calm surface of Hebgen Lake, Robert watched as more callibaetis hatched and hovered in their ascending and descending mating flight. The flesh of the callibaetis flies, being part of the trout, was also soon to become part of Robert's body and life energy. Never before had Robert perceived the insect as being important to his life. For him, this was an epiphany, and the depth and clarity of the revelation was stunning.

The intellectual and academic nature of the science was intriguing. However, the notion that a callibaetis fly is an integral part of a system much larger than human experience, had been lost on Robert until that magical moment on Hebgen Lake in Montana. Separateness, not oneness, had been the perception that Robert had always had of his surroundings.

Robert sat quietly in his canvas chair, looking at the trout fillets and watching the mating dance of the callibaetis above the surface of Hebgen Lake. Distant thunder awakened him from his trance, as the snow-capped mountains to the west began to disappear into the darkening clouds of an approaching rainstorm. Hazy gray streaks of rain were visible, and the surface of the lake dimpled with its first gentle drops. Again, Robert could see clearly the connections that he had not previously been conscious of. Over millions of years, rain had washed the mineral and alkaline content from the surrounding mountains into the lake, creating the precise environment necessary for callibaetis to live.

The rain was driven by the evaporative energy of the sun and wind, which were part of the sky, which Native peoples regarded as their Father. Robert had always taken the sky as separate from the earth, and had only contemplated it in a scientific and astronomical sense.

There was a knowingness that the sun and the mountains and the rain that were part of the callibaetis would, through the trout, soon become a

part of his own body. The realization of that oneness of all things brought
a peaceful smile of awakening to Robert's face.

■ ■ ■

Robert sat in the warm gentle rain with no thought of putting on his rain
gear or seeking shelter in his truck. From his chair, he gazed at a small
green plant with delicate purple flowers that grew out of the sandy soil. A
lone red ant crawled amongst the dried pine needles that had collected at
the base of the plant. Surely the ant, the sand, and the moisture in the sand
that was used by the plant, all contained the same sacred essence as did the
trout, the callibaetis, the mountains, and Robert.

Trying to find and identify the purple flowering plant in his wild-
flower field guide seemed almost meaningless. Experiencing the essence
of the plant was all that Robert needed at that moment. Surely, the life
energy locked within the atoms that formed the molecules and cells of all
things must have come, an eternity ago, from the same mysterious source.
The science concerning that source also seemed unimportant to Robert,
compared to experiencing its essence.

Robert's impulse was to pick the purple flowering plant in order to
show it to other people when he tried to explain to them what he had experienced. The trailing wind from the passing rainstorm blew through the
plant, and the flowers nodded as if to ask Robert, why it was necessary to
kill the plant and take it from its place in the universe in order to awaken
others to the oneness of all things.

■ ■ ■

Mist arose from the earth and the forest as the sun's heat energy rekindled
the evaporative process. The two rainbow trout fillets were cooked in olive oil to a crisp golden brown and were lying on Robert's tin plate. With
each nourishing bite of fish, Robert thought about what had happened to
him that morning. He thought about his life and his unconscious human
ego and arrogance. He realized the illusion of his old belief that he was

a separate and discrete entity. His purpose was no higher, and he was no more important to God than were the sun, the earth, the fish, the plants and insects—and indeed, all other things.

Robert knew that the natural world had given him a gift. He was certain he never would have made the connection between the universe and frozen fish wrapped in plastic that he purchased at the supermarket. American culture has sanitized the reality of food—where it comes from and how it is connected to something bigger than the grocery store. A society of people, removed from its source and the interconnectedness to all things, comes to believe the myth that they are indeed separate and autonomous. They live in that lonely place of fantasy, away from and above the fish, animals, the Earth Mother and Father Sky.

■ ■ ■

The osprey pair circled high in Montana's morning sky. One of the birds, with collapsing wings, plummeted into the quiet water of Hebgen Lake, emerging with a small trout struggling against the clasp of powerful talons—and another cycle of life and death and new life went flying toward the osprey's large nest, conspicuous in the top of a tall larch pine tree.

Robert and his yellow Labrador dog lingered on the shore of Hebgen, where Cherry Creek flows into the lake.

Looking out over the lake, Robert declared, "My understanding of how I fit into the world will never again be the same."

The sun was high and the wind gusted from the northwest. The callibaetis were gone but he knew they would be back to feed him and the trout.

Robert Peterson sat with his patient companion on the front seat of his pickup truck. Giving the dog's neck a long and loving hug, Robert knew that he was home.

COPPER JOHN

Robert felt a deep connection with John and the river community.…
He was experiencing serenity in his mind
and peace creeping into his body.

A small rainbow trout flashed its silvery side in the late afternoon sun-light as it chased an emerging black caddis fly. Turning to move further downriver, Robert noticed the motionless form of a man sitting with his back resting against a large cedar tree. The man was old. Very old. His red-and-black flannel shirt was worn through at the elbows, and the collar and cuffs were frayed from years of wear. Gray-and-white locks of long, dirty hair stuck out in various directions from under the sides and back of his brown felt hat.

As Robert approached, the old man did not seem to want to engage in conversation, and continued to stare at the river without a hint of move-ment in his body.

"How's fishin'?" Robert asked cheerily as he stepped closer to the squatted form. The afternoon breeze moved his gray tangled hair slightly, but the old man continued his trance-like stare into the river.

Feeling slightly annoyed by this lack of acknowledgement, Robert moved directly in front of the man and repeated loudly, "Doin' any good today?"

Slowly, the old man raised his head, locked his clear blue eyes with Robert's, and asked politely in a tone that was almost reverent, "What did you say?"

Exasperated, Robert asked in a slow, deliberate voice, "How-many-fish-have-you-caught-to-day?"

The man's deeply tanned and weathered hand moved slowly over the small pine cones and needles that littered the ground, coming to rest on an ancient-looking fiberglass fly rod lying beside him. The rod reminded Robert of the one that his father had purchased sixty-five years ago, upon returning home from World War II. The grip was stained nearly black, and a deep depression dented the cork handle, about where the fisherman's thumb would rest. Dental floss held the few remaining eyelets.

After an uncomfortably long silence, the old man opened his nearly toothless mouth and began to speak.

"The river provided me with two of her children today. I didn't catch them, but as I became part of the river community, two trout were offered to me. When you arrived, I was thanking the Great Spirit for this moment, and the beauty and energy of this place. The energy of the trout is now part of me, and I am grateful to the river, the trout, and the Great Spirit for these gifts."

Robert noticed the smoldering remains of a small cooking fire, and the sharpened willow sticks the man had used to skewer the trout's flesh.

"I apologize for interrupting your moment," Robert said softly. "Did you get them on black caddis? Were any of them good fish?"

The old man extended his right leg so he could reach deep into the pocket of his tan wading pants. Producing a small black-handled folding knife, he cut a generous corner piece from a rectangular block of tobacco. With eyes closed, he held some of the twisted offering above his head and allowed the wind to blow it from his opened palm.

"And so it is," he mumbled, slipping the remaining chew into the corner of his left cheek.

Robert noticed tiny streams of brown tobacco juice appear in both corners of the old man's mouth, and watched intently as they began to find their way down the deeply grooved channels of his wrinkled chin.

"My name is John. In town, they call me Copper John."

"Hello, John. My name is Robert. If you don't mind me asking, why do the people around here call you Copper John?"

"Well ya see, years ago, I was the first to tie a little red-and-copper-colored trout fly that's since become popular on the rivers out here. My nickname came out of that fly. You care to sit a while, or do you gotta go catch a fish?" asked the old man with a sly grin.

"I don't have much time left on my fishing trip. I only get three weeks of vacation a year. I suppose I could sit for a while, until the black caddis start to hatch. Then I'll have to go."

"Not many folks around these parts care to talk with me," John opened. "They think I'm schizophrenic or something—or at least eccentric and strange. And I hope I am strange—compared to them."

"There weren't any other vehicles in the parking area. How did you get way out here?"

"My bicycle is hidden in the weeds beyond those two big rocks. People in town think I'm crazy because I bike everywhere. Sometimes the kids try to scare me off the road by driving close, and honking and yelling that I should get a horse."

"Have you ever called the police on them?"

"For what?" John laughed. "I'm powerless over how quickly the kids grow up or don't grow up. Just like I'm powerless over how quickly the marsh marigolds bloom in the spring. The kids, Mother Earth, and the river have their own clocks."

An osprey's laugh interrupted the conversation, and Robert and Copper John watched the raptor glide gracefully onto its favorite fishing perch in a dead tree. John pointed his bent and arthritic index finger in the direction of the bird. He invited Robert to observe how the osprey flies into the wind to gain altitude, then with the wind to gain speed, and finally to plummet into the water, grasping for a fish.

"The river provides food for our brother osprey, with or without any black caddis. The birds seem to just know how to be a bird, to use the wind, to live off the trout, and to live with the river. They, too, are powerless over whether or not the black caddis will hatch today."

John leaned to his right and arced a long brownish-yellow stream of tobacco juice over his fly rod and onto a rotting log.

"Robert, how much time do you have left?" John asked pointedly.

"You mean to fish, or on my vacation? Or to get home, or in life, or what?" Robert asked as he sat down next to Copper John.

"I mean how much time is there between now and what you are going to do next?"

"I don't know for sure what I am going to do next," Robert stammered, "but whatever it is, I don't have much time to do it. I should be going somewhere soon, I think."

"Robert, listen to the water in the river. Listen to the wind in the branches of this cedar tree we're leaning against. The water is going where it is going to go. Have you ever tried to push against the river or the wind? No matter how hard we try, we can't change the outcome. We can't make the black caddis hatch, or stop the kids from running me and my bicycle off the road. We are just powerless over so many things."

Copper John adjusted his position, inhaled, and continued.

"You and I, Robert, are like the osprey coming back to the dead tree. We all have the same amount of time right now to be a bird, a man, a trout, a marigold, a black caddis fly. In this moment, Robert, we are all exactly the same age, with the same amount of time to live; one moment at a time. We are all part of the same sacred place and time, connected in a way the river seems to understand. She provides for all that are part of her.

"Robert, you must know that life only happens in the present moment. If you wait or imagine that you will only find peace and happiness in the future, you will never be happy or at peace. The best you can do is to hope that someday it will happen for you. In this moment, nobody has any more or less time or opportunity to live than anyone or anything else does."

Robert suddenly leapt to his feet, looking down on Copper John.

"I'm sixty-one years old, you must be at least ninety, and you say we're the same age?"

"No," John calmly replied. "I said we have the same amount of time to live life in this moment. This body has been home to my life energy and spirit for eighty-nine years, but right now, in this moment when life is happening—the only time when life has ever happened—you and I have exactly the same amount of time to either live life, or to miss it."

"And you say that the river *provides* the osprey and you and me with fish, we don't really catch them?"

"No, I said the fish and the bird and you and the river and I are all connected by energy that comes from the same sacred and mysterious source, and that the energy is moving in its destined direction, no matter how hard we fight or fish or push to make it move in a different way."

"And you say that you are powerless over the children in town and the marsh marigolds in the spring?"

"I said that I was powerless over how quickly the kids grow up, or when the marsh marigolds appear in the spring, or if the black caddis hatch or not. Some other power makes those decisions. You and I can either go along with those decisions or decide to fight them or wish they were different. Mother Nature will indeed have her way. Resisting is futile and will lead to frustration and unhappiness."

Copper John spit another stream, this one less brown and more yellow than the first, and closed his eyes to rest. Robert sat down next to John and felt the tree trunk slowly move with the wind's powerful force. He felt John's bony and atrophied eighty-nine-year-old shoulder resting on the muscles of his still strong sixty-one-year-old shoulder.

And then it became perfectly clear, Copper John was right! The only time we have is now—the present. If we truly know this, each moment becomes part of an eternity—a moment that never has been before and will never be repeated. This must be the "luminous pause" that Carl Jung described as "being one with the two great mysteries of the eternal past and future."

Robert recalled studying Jung in college. In his famous and enduring teachings, the renowned psychiatrist emphasizes the need for a direct spiritual awakening—an awareness and connection to something bigger than oneself, to something eternal and sacred. Without such an awakening, humans are "bound to encounter increasing neurotic difficulties."

Robert was at midlife, and he had no sense or belief about how he fit into anything bigger than himself, or what might happen after he died.

He had arrived in the Madison River Valley three weeks ago, filled with anxiety and worries about finances and his mother's health. The feelings of dread and disconnect were demons that he fought with daily.

But now Robert felt a deep connection with John and the river community, and he no longer felt old and desperate to accomplish grandiose feats. He was no longer in a hurry to get to as many places as possible, since he really didn't know where he was going or when he was supposed to get there. He was experiencing serenity in his mind and peace creeping into his body. Robert Peterson wondered if finally, after sixty-one years of life, he was experiencing his True Self—what Jung described as a "connection with spirit." It was mysterious, yet the connection felt so real, leaning against the cedar tree with Copper John.

■ ■ ■

The osprey lifted from its perch, and circled into the darkening evening sky. Robert noticed an adult black caddis fly crawling up the front of the old man's sweat-stained felt hat.

"John! Wake up! The black caddis hatch is on. There's another one! The sky is full of them. Let's get to the river and catch some trout."

Copper John smiled, opened his rested blue eyes, and stretched so that he could find the folding knife in his right pocket. Sixty-six years ago, his mother had given him that knife for good luck, just before he deployed to England, and eventually Normandy. John's little knife had opened hundreds of C-ration tins, was with him in Berlin as the war in Europe ended, and had helped steady his nerves as he was decorated an American war hero by the Secretary of the Army. His courage had helped defeat the enemies of freedom.

John thought about his mother's lovely smile and gentle tears, and her strong and loving arms that had hugged her only son farewell. Now, her voice was in the wind softly beckoning him, her tears were in the river, and her spirit came powerfully to Copper John.

"My mother is here with us, Robert. Would you mind if she came fishing with us this evening?"

"Of course she's welcome. Bring her along," Robert said, without thinking about the extraordinary words that had just tumbled from his mouth. "I'm feeling the river will be generous tonight."

Robert extended his hand to help Copper John to his feet. Although his knuckles and bones creaked and moaned as Robert pulled him up, John's grip was solid and firm. As their eyes met, Robert knew he would never again be the same man who had arrived in that place just three weeks ago.

Robert Peterson had realized a oneness with a war hero, whom teenagers mocked, and townspeople thought crazy. He now knew an old man who had humbly, without any conditions or expectations, shared the wisdom of a thousand years. He had met a generous river, which was once only a place to catch and photograph big trout. He had met a bird that he used to call "osprey," but now the bird felt more like a brother in a river community. And most important, in that transformative moment, Robert Peterson had finally met his True Self in the spirit living within him.

Copper John had taught him these lessons and shown him that the present moment is the only time when life happens. Robert knew that he was not his sixty-one-year-old body, or his thoughts, or his accomplishments, his net worth, career, or the number of big trout he caught. Robert knew that his True Self was the formless energy embodied within his physical form. And as his physical body weakened and ceased to function, the energy would mysteriously flow elsewhere into different and unknowable places and forms.

At middle age, Robert had come to a spiritual awakening and a belief that made him feel alive again—even reborn. Indeed, he was less fearful, and at peace with what was happening in the moment. Jung had been correct: The dreadful discontent and persistent fear of death and dying were diminishing.

■ ■ ■

Robert fished upstream, while Copper John and the spirit of his mother moved slowly downriver and eventually disappeared into the lengthening shadows of the evening. The black caddis hatched by the thousands, and Robert netted four trout—one rainbow measuring just over twenty-one inches long. Although he had his camera, he took no pictures. Instead, he felt gratitude for Copper John, the river, the trout, and the life-giving flow of energy moving around him and within him.

It was very late, but the trail to his truck was dimly lit by the nearly full August moon. As he felt his way around the two large boulders lying next to the trail, Robert tripped on John's hidden bicycle. He wondered if John was in danger. Was the old man okay? Should he go looking for his new friend?

Robert picked up John's precious bicycle and carefully leaned it against one of the rocks. He felt how the handlebar grips were worn smooth from decades of use. He thought about John's white hair blowing from beneath his felt hat as the kids from town tried to run him off the road and into the ditch. He felt the old man's forgiving heart and love, knowing how he patiently watched and waited for the kids to mature, and for the marigolds to open into the spring sunshine.

Turning toward the river and looking downstream into the darkness, Robert said, "You made it through D-day and Berlin and eighty-nine years of living, Copper John. You and your mother will be fine… wherever you are."

He knew the people in town probably would not miss John; they may not even have cared enough to come out and help look for him. But the river, the wind, the osprey, the trout, and his mother were all there singing, "Welcome home, Copper John."

■ ■ ■

The following summer, Robert returned to Montana's Madison River Valley. Unlike his custom in previous years, Robert resisted the urge to drive the 1300-mile trip straight through. He did not feel rushed to be anywhere except where he was during each moment and each mile of the long journey west.

He was aware of the steepness of the hills leading into and away from the ancient Mississippi River drainage. He was conscious of the peaceful and gentle nature of the South Dakota antelope that grazed along the highway. He inhaled and savored the rich aroma of hazelnut coffee being brewed at 2 a.m. in a truck stop near Sturgis, and spent time talking with the bored clerk whose young child slept behind the counter in a faded green chair.

Although Robert remembered Copper John's lessons about being mindful of the present moment, he couldn't wait to get to the river, and he speculated whether or not the black caddis would be hatching. The green-and-white road sign read "Welcome to Montana," and he pictured the Madison River Valley and the huge rainbow and brown trout that hungrily awaited his newly tied black caddis and Copper John flies.

There were no vehicles in the parking area, and the trail heading leading to the river was overgrown and appeared unused. Robert pulled on his wading boots, tied on a Copper John fly and headed down the trail toward the river. As he walked, Robert thought he could faintly hear the river's song calling to him. He saw the first and then the second big rock looming on the side of the trail. The osprey's scream called him a bit closer. And then, there it was. Copper John's rusted Schwinn bicycle, tipped over from the weight of last winter's snow, was lying next to the big rock, surrounded by the beauty of wild irises.

During the past year, in his heart, Robert had known that John and his mother had left this world together, but he had to return just to sit here for a while. Robert rested his back against one of the big rocks. The irises nodded their yellow heads as he closed his eyes to listen. A raven called contentedly from the top of a nearby cedar tree. The sparrows sang. The black caddis hatched.

Robert Peterson looked toward the sky and smiled.

"Hello, Copper John. I know you're here. Thank you for all the wisdom, and for being part of my life."

HIGH GROUND

I go fishing not to find myself, but to see myself.

—*Joseph Monniger*

A bird song floated across the inlet. The sweet, soothing music helped relax and heal my frayed nerves and weary mind. The High Ground, next to the inlet where the Madison River gently flows into Hebgen Lake, is a sacred place for me. I come here to find peace when the world is too loud and overwhelming. And I could not remember a time in my life when I felt more drained, and in need of peace.

My ninety-year-old mother had just died after valiantly fighting to recover from a stroke. All of her five children were present when the respiratory therapist slowly turned the breathing machine off, and the attending physician pronounced that my beautiful mother was dead. Without Dad, and now Mom, my world would never again be the same.

While still grieving the loss of my parents, I also was deciding if I should retire from my thirty-five-year teaching career as a professor of business and economics. I had won four prestigious university awards for excellence in teaching, made a comfortable and secure living, and had fifteen weeks a year to pursue other interests and passions. Why should I leave the familiar and secure career that kept me alive and comfortable? Will I feel that I'm unproductive—that I've lost myself? Will I be bored? Maybe I'll regret leaving the university. Maybe I'll miss being surrounded by interesting students and colleagues. Will I find another purpose in life?

There were more questions than answers, and my unsettled mind continued to grind away in painful rumination. My life was changing, but I was filled with fear and resistance to change. I kept hearing a voice deep within me saying, "Howard, there is something more."

■ ■ ■

Moving down the hill from High Ground to the inlet, I watched, then cautiously stalked, a large rainbow trout feeding quietly on tiny mayflies. The graceful and powerful fish moved silently through the water, methodically picking dead and dying flies from the smooth surface of the inlet.

With great delicacy, I cast my gray-and-white imitation mayfly six feet ahead of the huge trout. My heart raced as I waited for the fish to take my fly. The trout moved boldly toward the fly, and warily ascended. Every nerve and fiber of my muscle tissue was alive with anticipation of the strike, which never came—a "refusal," in the jargon of trout fishers. The trout's instinct for survival was too strong—or perhaps the monofilament leader attaching the fly to the fly rod was too visible.

I watched as the beautiful silver-and-pink trout disappeared into the security of the familiar depths of the inlet.

Climbing out of the inlet and up the hill to High Ground, my mind slipped back into its familiar groove of indecision, and fear of the unknown.

■ ■ ■

It was almost dark when I finished pitching my mountain tent on that special place I call High Ground. The night air was still, and unusually cold, and the Coleman lantern's warmth felt good on my chilled hands. Its soft light glowed in a warm circle on the tent floor, and Cody Ann, my five-year-old yellow Labrador, inched further into the circle.

"Hey Cody, listen to this one," I insisted, reading a quote written by the famous psychiatrist, Carl Jung.

"'A normal goal to a young person becomes a neurotic hindrance in old age.'"

At sixty, I wasn't sure if I was entering old age, but I certainly was no longer a young person.

Jung's four stages of life follow the progression of the human journey, from childhood, through first adulthood, into the middle passage, and finally, for some, into the spiritually centered newness of second adulthood. I had achieved the important and foundational first adulthood goals of finding my personal identity, obtaining financial security, achieving some prestige and social standing, finding loving companionship, having fulfilling employment, and owning material possessions. Jung's description of the middle passage did actually mirror the past ten years of my life. So was now the time to join the few who journey ever deeper into the unknown, spiritual realm of second adulthood?

■ ■ ■

Cody stretched her legs, stood up, circled counterclockwise three times, and collapsed with a groan into a new sleeping position. A nearby bird sang a single note of welcome to the new day. The lantern hissed and sputtered to darkness as the propane canister gave up its last gasp of fuel.

I stayed in my sleeping bag, watching the dawn arrive. As the first hint of pinkness appeared on the eastern horizon, it came to me. I must be in the final stages of the middle passage. The torment, depression, and sleepless nights were my Spirit calling to me, making its powerful invitation to a further journey. It would be a journey away from the callings of the world, and toward a life of deeper connection with Spirit—my authentic and True Self.

Cody jerked convulsively; her legs and paws moved as if she were running in some exciting dream. I was wide awake, and I knew my awareness was not a dream. Indeed, it was the gift of an awakening—it was the gift of grace.

Like the old rainbow trout that was invited to take the fly, I also was at a critical moment in my life. Would it be enough to successfully survive the remainder of my life? Or was there something more? Clearly, something mysterious and unknown was in store for me, and avoiding that something seemed to be at the root of my depression and loss of energy. Whatever that something was, it had been persistent, and it had been troubling me during many long and sleepless nights.

Now I finally knew what it was: my long-ignored, but always present, True Self. It was the Spirit within, calling me to a new meaning and purpose for my life—an urging to use the lessons of the first adulthood to move into a further journey.

For thousands of years, religious teachers, poets, philosophers, and spiritual guides have written and preached and taught the same message—coming home to the "Father within." Now was my time to either refuse or say yes to the summoning call for a further journey into an even richer, more meaningful life.

It felt like my life's purpose now was to have less to do with career or financial security, and more to do with answering spiritual callings—which had become relentless and very loud. Mary Oliver's poem, "The Journey," called it the day when "you knew what you had to do, and began." Take the risk, and trust and believe that the loving forces of the universe will provide the necessary guidance through the perilous, and often difficult, journey of second adulthood.

■ ■ ■

The morning sun moved higher in the big Montana sky, and finished its work of burning off the fog and mist from the Madison River Valley. I screwed a new canister of propane into the side of my camp stove, and fed Cody while waiting for the coffee water to boil. In my heart, I felt the stirrings of lightness and freedom—feelings that had been so elusive throughout the previous year.

An osprey whistled and chattered as it hovered, then dropped onto a dead tree to watch for fish. The river called me as I carefully picked my way down from the High Ground to the quietness of my fishing spot.

The osprey watched for fish and waited patiently. I thought about the wisdom of Father Richard Rohr, who in his book *Falling Upward*, wrote:

> *The way up is down. None of us go into spiritual maturity completely of our own accord, or totally by free choice. We are led by Mystery, which religious people rightly call grace.... Setting out is always a leap of faith, a risk, yet an adventure.*

The first small mayfly magically appeared on the inlet's smooth surface, and then another. Soon there were thousands, floating and flying, then dropping back to the water and ascending again and again. As I watched, spellbound, the words of other authors entered my mind.

Father Thomas Merton wrote, "We may spend our whole life climbing the ladder of success, only to find when we get to the top, that our ladder is leaning against the wrong wall."

And Scott Peck, author of *The Road Less Traveled*, offered, "Most people are spiritually lazy. And when we are lazy, we stay on the path we are already on, even if it is going nowhere."

The osprey's scream startled me from my contemplative moment, and I watched the bird plummet from the sky, emerging from the quiet water with a small trout fighting desperately against the grip of deadly talons. And then I heard them—trout feeding on mayflies all around me. Time to go fishing—perhaps for the same smart old rainbow trout that refused my fly the day before.

Maybe a less visible leader and a larger fly would fool the wise and wary old fish. I could hear the faint sound of a trout feeding in the same location where the rainbow had been. My heart pounded and my hands fumbled with the knots and dry-fly dressing. The knots were strong, my breathing steadied—I was ready.

The big trout had settled into a steady and predictable feeding rhythm. The timing and spacing of my cast was as perfectly and naturally present-ed as my casting skills allowed. The big rainbow stayed on course to the fly, and I tried desperately to control my spiking adrenaline.

"Don't set the hook too fast," I whispered through shallow breathing. "And don't pull too hard and break the light leader."

The glistening black nose of the trout appeared three feet from the fly, and I could see the white insides of his mouth as he ate a struggling mayfly. The big trout's gill covers flared, and my fly disappeared from the surface of the inlet.

I lifted the fly rod gently while pulling ever so lightly on the fly line. Instantly, the power and fury and defiance of the hooked fish exploded onto the surface of the inlet. He had made a mistake, and his survival instincts screamed, *Get to deeper water! Find a submerged log or limbs to hide in; your life depends on it!*

Slowly stepping back toward the shore, I firmly guided the frantic fish away from the snags and rocks, where it desperately sought escape and refuge. The relentless arc and even pressure of the fly rod was beginning to drain the terrific power from the trout's body. I marveled at the stunningly beautiful coloration of the fish in the gin-clear water of the inlet. God was here for sure, and I was overcome with awareness and gratitude for it all.

The trout lay in the water, corralled by the wooden frame of my net. The fish was completely exhausted. There was no more fight, only surrender. I carefully removed the fly from the corner of its mouth. Seemingly unaware that he was free, the trout's right eye stared at me, in resignation. For a moment, I felt a deep empathic connection with the subdued fish, as I only recently was becoming aware of my own freedom—from the tyranny of instinct and fear. With gentle urging, the big rainbow trout swam, slowly at first, and then with a burst of speed into the safety of the inlet.

I knew that both I and the trout had just learned life lessons—but in very different ways. I had options and life-changing choices to make. The trout's life, driven by instinct alone, would fundamentally not change. His life was locked into feeding on insects, and living in the safety of the inlet. For him, there was no alternative.

From the High Ground, I looked down at the inlet, and appreciated how amazingly "blessed and highly favored" we humans really are! Instead of being completely controlled and limited by instincts, we can override and transcend our instinctual behavior, and make life choices on other criteria such as intuition, probability, evaluation, logic, and spiritual calling. Just safely surviving becomes limiting—we can have more. And perhaps the universe, in return for these special gifts, expects more from us as a species.

For sure, I could continue to survive and be safe by staying on the "same path even if it is going nowhere." But, is that enough for a human who has the capacity, and the calling, to transcend instincts, and go deeper into the mystical spiritual depths of life? We are "highly favored" as a species, and to not use these gifts seems to run contrary to the principle of balance in natural law.

Yes, the time was right, and I was ripe to make a change, to "lean my ladder against the right wall"—the further journey into the spiritual realm of second adulthood.

■ ■ ■

Cody Ann followed my scent trail to the river, and she searched with her nose for clues to what might have happened there. The sun was high, and Cody swam aimlessly in the coolness of the inlet. After carefully stowing the tent and my fishing equipment, I started the truck for the long journey home. At the sound of the engine, Cody ran up the hill to the truck, wet and happy.

Opening the back door, I called, "Load up, Cody, it's time to go home. School starts in a week, and I've got a letter of resignation to write."

PART 4: COMING HOME

What is a normal goal to a young person becomes
a neurotic hindrance in old age.

—Carl Jung

The passage into old age is another very difficult part of life's journey. Fear of getting old and dying causes many of us to circle back into the confusion, rationalizing that we feel lost and empty because we just haven't acquired quite enough stuff to make us happy. After a lifetime of believing the dream, it's difficult to let it go.

Our survival instincts instruct us to keep doing what has kept us alive—even if our lives seem to be going nowhere. Mesmerized by chasing society's rabbits, we may be unaware that alternative paths to happiness and serenity even exist. But in life's final stage, there are some who will choose to take the risk of traveling in a new direction, finally on a journey that is in alignment with their own Spirit. This is the road less traveled.

Other people's plans were not working for me. The new direction I chose had almost nothing to do with financial security, prestige, or material things, and everything to do with finding more meaning and purpose in my life. I am grateful for the urgings of my Spirit, the wisdom of the

Earth Mother, and the love of my dogs, as they guide me now on my journey home.

In this part of the book, you will read about how a walnut tree awakened me to the reality that I am now an elder, and no longer a warrior. You will meet the dog who taught me how to forgive, and feel the powerful healing that act of love can bestow. And you will share in a truly amazing gift of forgiveness, given to me while I was on a Big Horn River vision quest. Finally, the last story in this book, appropriately titled "The Last Dog," brings this journey to a conclusion, at the special place on this Earth that was meant for me, and for the dogs that have shared my life.

THE WALNUT TREE: FROM WARRIOR TO ELDER

Don't judge each day by the harvest you reap
but by the seeds that you plant.

—*Robert Louis Stevenson*

Cody whined impatiently as the truck came to a stop in the overgrown yard. Robert grimaced as he stiffly emerged from the truck. Three deer nervously watched their arrival, then disappeared into the woods behind the barn. It felt good to be home after six weeks of camping and trout fishing in Montana's mountains.

Robert's kitchen was a welcoming place. Cody got reacquainted with her food bowl and dog bed, while Robert stared blankly into the nearly empty refrigerator. The flashing red light on the answering machine indicated its memory was full.

The house keys still dangled from the door lock when the kitchen phone began to ring.

"Hello Robert, it's Tom. I've been calling for two weeks, but you never return my calls."

"I've been in the mountains for six weeks. What's up?"

"Saturday, about twenty of us are traveling to northern Wisconsin to protest against a proposed open-pit taconite mine. Big business has the governor sniffing at their check books again, and we have to fight these bastards hard—they just won't quit!"

Robert felt six weeks of accumulated peace and serenity begin to drain from his body and mind.

"Let me think about it, Tom."

"No time for thinking; we have to be doing. The greed and environmental exploitation must be stopped now. We are warriors, Robert, and warriors must fight!"

"I'll think about it" Robert repeated, and hung up.

Cody appeared in the kitchen with a tattered fabric duck in her mouth that made a tantalizing quack as she repositioned the toy between her teeth. Her raised ears and pleading eyes begged, "Will you please throw this for me? It's been a long time since I've chased a duck!" Cody scrambled after her prize as Robert tossed the duck into the cluttered living room. He marveled at the enthusiasm and simplicity of her life, and he longed for more of those qualities in his own life.

Robert sat quietly in the green reclining chair that was located in the middle of his kitchen. He was aware that a shift had been occurring within him, and he asked Cody, "Do I really need to fight against big business and a strip mine? I've been fighting against real estate developers and big corporations for thirty years without much success, and I am just not into that anymore."

Sleep came easily as Robert lay back into the green chair. After dozing for a time, Robert became aware that the fabric duck, soaked from its time in Cody's mouth, was again resting on his lap. Opening one eye, he met Cody's intense stare, telegraphing her hope for another chance to chase the magical quacking duck.

"Go lay down Cody, I need some time to be alone and think."

■ ■ ■

It was late afternoon, and Robert dreaded the prospect of unloading the truck. Instead, it seemed a much better idea to make a batch of his favorite cookies—walnut chocolate chip. It had been over three decades since he and his brother had transplanted a small walnut tree from his mother's yard to a secluded meadow on his farm. Robert was aware that the tree was still alive, but in all those years, he had never returned to the transplant site. The possibility of enjoying fresh walnuts in the chocolate chip cookies was reason enough to hike to the tree, and hopefully gather some walnuts.

The sumac leaves had turned bright red while Robert and Cody had been in Montana. Surging ahead on the path leading to the walnut tree, Cody startled a doe and her fawn in a field of big blue stem and Indian grass. Robert watched, mesmerized by the speed and graceful bounds of the deer and noticed that they too had exchanged their summer color for the brown and gray of autumn. The family of geese that had hatched in the pond near the house had completed their molt and were flying in formation to feed in a nearby wheat field.

The natural world was again changing, and so was Robert Peterson. Both his father and mother had recently made their transitions to the mysteries of another realm, and he missed them both as he and Cody climbed the hill to the meadow and the walnut tree.

Evening sunlight played its color magic as Robert watched the kaleidoscope of hues move through the waving prairie grass. He was amazed as he approached the walnut tree. From a small sapling in search of a home, the tree had grown to well over thirty feet tall. Robert was delighted to discover hundreds of yellow-and-brown walnuts littering the ground beneath the tree's sturdy limbs. He looked into a robin's nest that was built in the fork of a low-hanging branch and wondered how many fledgling birds had fluttered out of the walnut tree over the years. A few clusters of walnuts still clung to the tree, and Robert glimpsed a gray squirrel as it quickly moved behind a branch, and flattened itself to hide from the danger that was staring up at him.

Transplanting one small tree thirty-one years ago truly had changed the world in a profoundly positive way. Robert was in awe of the enormous contribution a single tree can make to the Earth and the life it sustains. A contented smile crept across his face as he began to gather walnuts. He knew they would soon be part of him when he ate warm cookies later that evening.

Sunlight dissolved into twilight as Robert walked to a high spot in the meadow to whistle for Cody. There, he noticed the first young walnut tree, and then another, and another. There were dozens of them scattered across the meadow! Some were over ten feet tall, and were maturing into healthy, life-giving citizens of the meadow. The work Robert and his brother had started, was continued for three decades by the earth, the sun, the rain, and the squirrels.

Cody stayed close to Robert's side as they walked in darkness toward the house.

"It's a miracle, Cody. I didn't have to fight against anything or anyone, and look what happened in the meadow. My brother and I transplanted one walnut tree thirty-one years ago, and then we just let it be."

The motion-sensing yard light clicked on as Robert and Cody approached the darkened house. In the kitchen, Robert reflexively answered the phone on its first ring.

"Hey Robert, it's Tom. We'll pick you up at 8 A.M. We've got twenty-seven people, and we need your help."

"I'm not going on this one, Tom. The fight is out of me. I really don't want to die an angry and frustrated old man."

"Are you planning to die soon?" Tom asked sarcastically.

"I have no idea how many days or years I have left, but I want my remaining time to be peaceful, and to be helpful in new ways."

"What in the hell happened to you in Montana?" Tom asked with a weak laugh. "I am just not getting through to you, am I?"

"I've changed Tom. I am no longer the warrior I used to be. Like the rivers in Montana, I just want to be free. I really don't know how things 'should be,' Tom. Do you?"

Robert could hear Tom breathing heavily and waited anxiously for the reply—which never came.

Robert had come home to his kitchen, the yard, the meadow, and to the walnut tree. But more important, he had come home to his true and authentic self. He was indeed ready to rest in the simplicity of life, and to be grateful for his small part in the universe. He was free to move with the truth of his changing nature—from the fighting and doing of his warrior years, to the quiet wisdom of being an elder. It worked beautifully for the walnut tree, and Robert was ready to allow Spirit to work in his life as well. He had changed—he felt it in his bones. He was finally home, and at peace.

■ ■ ■

The green reclining chair squeaked as Robert laid back and contemplated other places on the farm where he could transplant some of the young walnut trees that were growing in the meadow. And then there was a new voice coming from within him. The message was clear: *Robert, you have more to plant than walnut trees.*

Yes, of course—there are kind words to plant with strangers and friends, encouragement for Tom and his warriors, and forgiveness to be planted in the resentments still plaguing his tired mind. Compassion and consideration, and listening and touch, all were there for Robert to sow in a world desperately in need of them. And yes, seeds of peace and connection and love were also within Robert. He could either say yes, and humbly plant them as gifts to the world, or go back to the angry battles of his warrior years.

■ ■ ■

The smell of fresh walnut chocolate chip cookies filled the kitchen as they cooled on the window sill. Robert, relieved and happy he was not going to the protest, savored the distinctive bitter-sweet taste as he ate his first cookie. Cody appeared in the kitchen and quickly dropped the duck so that her mouth would be ready for cookie crumbs that might fall on the carpet.

With a smile of contentment, Robert said, "Come here, girl, we need to get some sleep. Tomorrow's a new beginning, and we've got lots of planting to do."

CLANCY'S GIFT

The memory of Clancy's gentle and forgiving
nature was alive and in my heart.
It was just not the time for judgment and revenge.

There were no tears left in my eyes. Brushing fresh dirt from my hands, I looked skyward for help. I asked the Great Spirit to receive the spirit and life energy of Clancy Girl, my yellow Labrador retriever. Clancy was a friend, a life companion, and the dog that I had lived with and loved for fourteen-and-a-half years.

Before we buried her body, Clancy's nine-year-old daughter, Little Maggie, and I sat by the gravesite and said our goodbyes. Maggie circled her mother and cautiously sniffed the sheet that she was wrapped in. I laid my hands on Clancy and recited the poem that I say to my dogs, when their dying time has come:

> *It came to me that every time I lose a dog, they take a piece of my heart*
> *with them; and every new dog who comes into my life gifts me with a*
> *piece of their heart. If I live long enough, all of the components of my*
> *heart will be dog, and I will become as generous and loving as they are.*

—Anonymous

. . .

It had been only thirty hours since Clancy had suffered a stroke. Clancy and Maggie and I had been on our traditional month-long trout-fishing trip to Montana. While I fished for trout, the dogs had chased each other and swum in the shallow water of Montana's Bighorn River.

That evening, while I was preparing dinner, Clancy pressed her body tightly against my right leg. With panic in her eyes, she looked to me for help and reassurance.

"What's wrong, old girl?" I asked, as she listed to the right and fell clumsily to the ground.

She tried valiantly to get up, but she careened out of control, crashing into the door of the truck and collapsing.

Dazed, Clancy lay in the dirt and pine needles, breathing heavily as her body trembled and her legs stiffened. She seemed glad to be held and stroked, but her eyes and my intuition told me that she was probably dying.

We lay together throughout the night, and I tried to comfort her and keep her warm. Clancy's time was close. It was not in my heart to wait for her to die, and then to bury my beautiful friend in an unmarked grave a thousand miles from home. I knew Clancy might well not make it home alive, but we were going to try.

Peace would come to her in the place where she had hunted ducks and geese in the cattails, rolled in the grass with Maggie and me, and slept by the wood stove on cold winter nights. Home—the place that she loved—the only place that was right for her to die.

We made it home. And that morning, as all three of us lay together in the yard, Clancy died to the sweet music of wild geese as they flew over to feed in a nearby wheat field. Clancy died at her home, at peace, with her pack. What more could any person, or dog, ask for? Her essence was gentleness, love, and forgiveness. She will live in my heart and bones forever.

■ ■ ■

Prior to our departure for the trip west, Brian, a new neighbor, had stopped in to say goodbye and wish me well. Brian is considerably younger than me, and I was grateful for the help he had given me with chores I can no longer do alone.

"You and the dogs have a great trip! Be safe; and I can't wait to hear stories about your adventures in the mountains."

"Thanks Brian. The dogs and I wait all year for this trip. Keep an eye on the place while I'm gone, and we'll see you in a month."

Our unexpected return home after being gone for only four days, would be a surprise to many people. With Clancy buried, Maggie and I returned to the house to rest and call Brian.

"Hello Brian, guess where I am?"

"You're on a mountain stream with Clancy and Maggie, catching monster rainbow trout?"

"No, sorry to say, I'm not. Clancy died this morning. Maggie and I just buried her behind the tractor shed."

After a long and uneasy silence, Brian whispered, "I am so sorry. She seemed fine four days ago."

"It's hard for me to talk about it right now. Stop by after work and we'll go out for dinner—in honor of Clancy Girl."

■ ■ ■

Maggie lay sprawled on the kitchen floor, enjoying the coolness of the linoleum. Her ears twitched and shuddered in annoyance at the relentless flies that were determined to land on her.

"Come on, Maggie," I urged. "Let's take a walk to the boat landing. I need to get out of the house."

Running down the steps into the yard, Maggie stopped abruptly and looked back at the house as if she was waiting for Clancy. After a while, with ears down and tail low, she returned to where we had buried Clancy earlier that day. My eyes welled with tears and my heart ached as Maggie searched in vain for signs of her missing mother.

Startled grasshoppers buzzed and flew in all directions as Maggie and I slowly walked the familiar trail toward the lake and boat landing. How different, how strange, even lonely, the walk was without Clancy's enthusiastic and happy company.

The afternoon sun was stiflingly hot, and I stopped to rest in the welcoming shade of a large oak tree. Suddenly, Maggie growled and barked excitedly at some animal that was snarling at her from beneath a nearby broken-down barbed wire fence.

"Maggie, here!" I commanded, running toward the angry commotion. And then, there it was. A large raccoon with a low and menacing growl, glaring at Maggie and me from behind the bars of a live trap. Holding Maggie's collar, we stared back and watched as the big animal struggled to turn around in the small cage.

"My God, Maggie, that's Brian's live trap; he promised he wouldn't do this."

My mind rewound back to the conversation Brian and I had just prior to my leaving for Montana. Brian had asked permission to live trap raccoons on my farm. He said he was training young hounds for raccoon hunting, and he needed live raccoons to fight with the dogs while they were both locked in large, rotating steel barrels. My answer was very clear.

"No. That training technique sounds horribly cruel to both the dogs and the raccoons. Besides, if you took a female in late summer, her young would likely suffer a slow and miserable death without their mother."

Brian had smiled, shrugged, and said he would get raccoons elsewhere.

My legs were trembling with weakness, and a hollow and sickening nausea descended into my gut.

"I just can't believe this Maggie. Brian promised not to do this!"

I felt an urgent need to free the animal from its confinement. Tying Maggie to the old fence, I quietly returned and knelt next to the trap. The raccoon's gray and black flanks heaved as she panted rhythmically in the hot sun. When she turned, her swollen mammaries protruded from beneath her belly and hind legs. I wondered if her babies were hiding nearby, hungry and frightened.

Her gaze was fixed as she stared down the trail leading to the boat landing. Maybe that's where her young were waiting, their lives and survival dependent upon their mother's return. Her initial defiance had given way to acceptance of her plight. She had surrendered. Her fate was in the hands of another, one who had more power and control over her life than she did.

Maggie sat quietly tethered to the old rusted fence. For just a moment my heart leapt as she appeared to be the exact image of her mother.

"Clancy, old girl, you haven't left us yet," I whispered. "Your spirit—you—are still here. I can feel your gentle and forgiving nature with us now."

Maggie turned her head and attention toward our old duck-hunting blind hidden in the cattails near the lake. She had lost interest in the raccoon. Instead, she was focused on the alarm calls of a flock of wild Canadian geese. Something invisible to me was chasing the geese off the lake. They left with noisy splashing and loud honks of protest. Clancy must just be having some fun chasing the geese, I mused with a smile.

With a stout branch, I carefully lifted the latch on the trap and raised the door. Hesitating for a moment, the mother raccoon looked at me, took one tentative step forward, then rocketed out of the trap and down the trail toward the boat landing.

The door dropped shut with a metallic clang, and Brian's trap was empty. Maggie was still staring at the duck blind when I untied her from the fence.

Giving her a big hug I exclaimed, "Maggie, now I know what I have to do!"

On my way back to the house, I stopped again in the shade of the big oak tree. The image of Brian's trap triggered an angry impulse to condemn him for his betrayal of me, our friendship, and his promise. My mind raced in an orgy of judgment and victimization. Setting the trap, thinking that he had a month to catch raccoons, was sneaky and deceitful. How could I ever trust him again?

Perhaps it was my moral duty to warn others of Brian's duplicitous nature, and rally them to support and encourage my self-righteous indignation. My mind tried hard to conclude that Brian was not worthy of my friendship, and that I must withhold it from him for my own safety and wellbeing.

In the judgment of the reptilian part of my brain, Brian was guilty. His sentence would be that I would shun him and not speak to him for a long time—perhaps forever! My primitive instincts were urging that he must be ostracized, banished from the tribe; he was dangerous and unpredictable.

But on that day, the fresh memory of Clancy's gentle and forgiving nature was everywhere. It was in the oak tree, the raccoon, and the bird song; it was in Maggie; and it was in my heart and spirit. It was just not the time for judgment and revenge. Clancy's body was buried in the earth, but she was with me in her compassionate and forgiving spirit.

The love and light that Clancy Girl had brought into my life was alive. I knew what I had to do. I would honor Clancy's life, in any way possible, choosing to practice kindness, love, and forgiveness in my life.

■ ■ ■

Maggie was lying in the cool dirt underneath the picnic table when Brian's truck turned into the driveway. We gave each other a hug.

"Thanks for being here for me, Brian. Let's sit at the picnic table in the shade of the willow tree."

"I'm sorry about Clancy. What happened?"

We talked about the events from the Bighorn River, the trip home, and our final hours together in the yard. I was grateful to have a friend who could share my emotions and pain.

"Maggie has been looking for her mother all day. After we buried Clancy, we walked to the boat landing, and Maggie kept looking up the trail, waiting for Clancy to join us."

Brian shifted nervously on the other side of the picnic table and gazed in the direction of the boat landing and barbed wire fence.

"Any geese on the lake?" he asked in a distracted voice.

"There was a small flock near the cattails. Maggie kept watching in that direction, and they all mysteriously flew. I believe Clancy chased them off. She loved to do that."

"Maybe so. I'm starting to half believe in that crazy stuff myself—or maybe it's just another strange coincidence."

Brian went silent for a long while. He seemed to be searching for a way to tell me something.

Suddenly he blurted, "Wanna play a game of cribbage? It'll get your mind off Clancy."

"Let's just sit for a while more," I replied. "How's the dog training coming along?"

"Okay, well ah, I haven't, ah..."

Brian hesitated, then looked away.

"I'm going to start training when I get a coon."

Maggie shifted her position under the picnic table, and dug deeper into the earth in search of cooler dirt. I felt totally at peace as our eyes locked. Brian put his head down on the picnic table.

In a small, hollow voice, he said, "You know about the trap, what can I do to fix this? I feel just sick."

"There is nothing to fix," I replied. "There are only valuable lessons to be learned by both of us. Let's do this together and honor the spirit of Clancy Girl."

"But I lied to you. I betrayed and deceived you. You're my friend—you trusted me and you've helped me."

"I've done all of those things in my life, and may well do them again. And as my friend, I'm counting on your help and understanding if and when they happen again. Our dogs are so forgiving, and in this way, we can choose to be like them. When they die, they leave these gifts in our hearts. Let's honor them by practicing kindness and forgiveness in our lives every chance we get!"

Brian's head remained in his folded arms on the picnic table. He appeared to be quietly sobbing as his shoulders convulsed and his head rolled side to side.

"Tell me what you think of this idea, Brian. You talk with somebody you trust and respect. Tell them the whole story in detail, leaving nothing out. Talk about your thoughts and actions, and how you are feeling now.

Ask for their ideas and suggestions. In one week, we'll meet right here and talk again."

"I'll do it," Brian promised. "I'll do anything you ask of me!"

I also shared with Brian what I had experienced with the mother raccoon. We both hoped that she was reunited with her young, sleeping together somewhere in a hollow tree.

Brian did not train his coon hounds that fall. Instead, he sold them to a hunter in Kentucky, and he hasn't hunted raccoons since.

When we talked again a week later, Brian and I agreed that the forgiveness that Clancy had awakened within us should be passed on to others. We must "pay it forward."

We also talked about trying to extend the awareness and compassion we felt when Clancy died, to our way of being in the world every day. Brian and I agreed that as friends, we must often remind each other of these lessons—that's what friends do for each other.

We have given each other permission to speak of these events, and the gifts and lessons that Clancy brought to us. Brian gave his permission and encouraged the writing of this story. Once, while he was speaking in public, I heard Brian tell the story of the raccoon trap. He used the story to illustrate forgiveness, and learning lessons from difficult life experiences.

■ ■ ■

On the day that Clancy died, and I discovered Brian's raccoon trap, my choices were clear. I could condemn, judge, punish, and reject Brian as a friend. Or I could recognize the similarities and brokenness in us both, and choose to practice forgiveness, instead of claiming victimhood and living with its toxic resentments.

Clancy's spirit seemed to be guiding my choices that day. With the melancholy I was experiencing, it was impossible not to be forgiving and merciful.

The forgiveness dividend for me during the past ten years has been the company and friendship of a wonderfully generous and kind human being. Brian also has chosen the path of helping others, and trying to make the world a kinder and more forgiving place.

Brian and I fish, golf, talk about life, and share secrets of the heart with each other. We have connected at the level of Spirit. Our friendship has enriched my life beyond measure, and I have grown spiritually in directions and dimensions that would not have happened if, on the day that Clancy died, I had chosen hatred over love, and darkness over light.

Thank you, Clancy Girl. I still miss you and Maggie.

SPIRIT BEAR

Forgiveness is the fragrance that a violet sheds
onto the heel of the boot that crushed it.

—*Mark Twain*

The silence of the Alaskan wilderness hummed in my ears as I watched the great bear methodically search the tundra for blueberries. His shiny black coat glistened in the September afternoon sun—he must have had a good summer. I saw the power in his thick five-hundred-pound body, and watched him move and flow with the ancient rhythms of this wild place—his home.

My senses ran fast and sharp—I was the predator—waiting silently, patiently, for him to come. Adrenaline pumped, and the yellow-and-orange fletched arrow, securely knocked on the string of my bow, jumped with each contraction of my heart.

Ancient hunters also waited in ambush, hoping to kill great beasts with their stone-tipped spears and arrows. Trembling limbs, shallow breathing, and pounding hearts, are links navigating backwards in time, connecting me to men who were both the hunter and the hunted, seekers of meat, as well as being sought for meat.

Will the hunt result in a kill? Will the family eat and the tribe survive, or will they starve into weakness, and ultimately disappear? Will the hunter be knocked to the ground by an enraged animal and be eaten alive while hopelessly struggling to inflict a mortal wound into the beast?

The hump in the bear's back, where his powerful shoulders join the rest of his body, appeared first. On he came, moving slowly but deliberately toward the small patch of willow brush where I crouched in ambush. Pulsating with fear, my mind and body struggled for composure and control.

The range calculator in my brain estimated his distance: Sixty yards. Fifty. Forty. Now, at thirty-five yards, his head suddenly snapped to attention. He stared in my direction, searching with his nose, his ears, and his eyes. Something was out of place. He sensed something was wrong—danger was nearby. Cautiously, he assessed the surrounding terrain. A blueberry bush that had been hanging from the left side of his mouth, dropped to the tundra.

It was then I first saw it—the half-dollar-sized shiny scar that covered the place where his right eye used to be. My mind conjured a loud and violent fight erupting on the mountainside. A claw or antler hooked the bear's right eyeball, laying it painful and bloodied onto his enraged and snarling face.

A raven's chattering redirected my focus, and distracted the bear long enough for me to draw my bow. I concentrated on a spot just behind his right shoulder. "Come on now," I whispered. "Visualize, exhale, release." And then the deadly orange-and-yellow fletched arrow was sailing on its final mission, sinking with lethal efficiency deep into his massive chest. With one final and defiant roar, the bear crashed wildly through a thick stand of willows, collapsing into the silence of his deathbed.

It was over. The tribe will dance and feast to honor the spirit of the bear. The meat will be shared, and songs of praise will be sung to Wakan Tanka—the Great Spirit. Prayers will be said, asking that the life energy of the bear's flesh be used by the people in ways that are good.

While skinning the bear, my hunting companion and I marveled at the brightness of the scar tissue that had replaced the bear's right eye. When the task was completed, I felt a heavy sadness for the great bear. From a noble presence on the tundra, he was reduced to piles of meat, body parts, a hide, and a head—with its haunting, never-closing, scarred right eye.

"I'll never do this again. This is the first and last bear I'll ever kill," I stammered as we shouldered meat-filled packs, and trudged up the mountain to our camp.

The bear's meat was shared with many grateful people. His hide was tanned and made into a rug that lies motionless in my living room. Sometimes, it feels as if he's just resting, waiting patiently for something to happen. His head looks the same as it did when he was alive in Alaska. But now, his eyes are made of glass, and they stare tirelessly through the patio doors, into the woods that surround my home.

Seventeen years after killing the one-eyed bear, I still occasionally knelt by his side in silence, reverently stroking his glistening black hair. Staring into his lifeless glass eyes, I wondered, "Why does the memory of killing you still haunt me? Why does this heavy sadness still reside deep within my heart?"

■ ■ ■

Montana's Bighorn River winds through desolate mesas and valleys of the Crow Indian Reservation. The historic Battle of the Little Bighorn, between General Custer's Seventh Cavalry and a large encampment of Lakota and Northern Cheyenne Indians, made the Bighorn River area a sacred place for many Native people.

Prior to the battle, and well before the Indians were aware of Custer's presence in the area, Sitting Bull, a Lakota Chief, received a sign from the spirit world while he was on a vision quest. Sitting Bull saw "pony soldiers" falling upside down from the sky to their deaths.

During a Council of Chiefs, Sitting Bull revealed his vision to other chiefs, such as Crazy Horse and Gall. When the pony soldiers launched a surprise attack against the village, the chiefs and warriors did not run or retreat, since they had been inspired and given courage by the spirit world's message of victory against the white enemy.

■ ■ ■

The world felt foreign, and unusually hostile to me. I was battling the enemy of depression, and desperately needed a vision for meaning and purpose in my life. I prayed hard to my spirit guides, who, I believe, travel in a nearby, but veiled, spirit world. But no medicine came.

Two Native American friends who practice their tribe's spiritual traditions and ceremonies in their own lives, suggested I go on a vision quest in a place that is sacred to me. The spirit world's energy feels strong in and around Montana's Bighorn River. The river called to me, and I knew the Bighorn was the place where my spirit guides wanted me to connect with their world.

The river knows me. For many years, I have felt a powerful connection with it. Fishing its trout and camping on the river's banks have been important times for me during the healing moon of August. And I was open and ready for a healing.

■ ■ ■

It was a warm and breezy August afternoon. Small mayflies emerged and floated on the surface of a quiet Bighorn River back-eddy. Brown and rainbow trout eagerly gulped their favorite late-summer meal.

Standing in the clear, cold river, I welcomed the peace that was finally finding its way into my weary and tormented mind. An osprey chattered from a nearby dead tree, and together, we waited and watched for trout.

The osprey scored first. Dropping from his perch with deadly speed, he reached into the water, emerging with a squirming trout firmly impaled on his hooked talons.

After the pool had settled from the osprey's disturbance, I caught two fat brown trout on two successive casts, filleting one for my evening meal.

Since I had no tobacco as an offering to the spirits for the gift of the fish, I ceremoniously laid its carcass under a wild olive tree growing on a nearby island.

The following morning, I paddled my kayak to the island to video the beauty and capture the serenity of the place. The trout offering lay undisturbed underneath the olive tree. Surprisingly, a raccoon or turtle or gull had not yet found the remains of the fish. Turning to leave the island, I noticed the movement of a large animal in the thick undergrowth. It was on the opposite side of a shallow channel of water running between the island and the steeply sloped bank of the river. Branches cracked and snapped as a black bear emerged from the brush, climbing calmly to the top of a small hill, seventy-five yards away.

Dropping to one knee, I videoed the bear as he looked down at me. It was exhilarating to video only the second bear I had ever seen in the wild. The first encounter was the one-eyed bear in Alaska—exactly seventeen years before.

The bear slowly moved down the hill, angling in my direction. Occasionally, he lifted his nose, clearly aware of my scent.

With the camera still running, I panned the brush, hoping to get one last picture of the bear. Suddenly, he emerged forty yards away on the opposite side of the channel. Crouching motionless in the shade of the olive tree, my body pulsated with fear. I struggled to find the courage to stay and video the majestic creature that had entered the channel and was walking directly at me.

My inner range calculator kicked in, estimating his distance to be thirty-five yards—the distance from which I had released the arrow that killed the bear in Alaska. The bear stopped in the middle of the channel as I loudly said, "Hey, who are you? What's your name?"

Searching with his nose and ears and eyes, he stood in the channel, as the swift water rushed noisily around and past his powerful legs. Midday sunlight danced on the water and reflected off the healthy luster of his jet-black hair. Nothing seemed wrong or dangerous to him, so on he came. Hoping to chase him back across the channel, I yelled in a frightened and shaky voice, "Hey you, I'm over here, what do you want?"

The bear turned his head slightly to the left, and then I saw it—a half-dollar-sized shiny scar covering the place where his right eye used to be. My mind reeled as I stammered, "My God, It's the spirit of the bear I killed in Alaska." The video camera kept running.

When he was at fifteen yards, I stood and backed away, angling toward my kayak, which was beached on the opposite side of the island. Stumbling as I backed over a vine-covered log, I dropped the video camera into a patch of willow brush and tall grass. Scrambling back onto my feet, I stood face to face with the bear. He stared at me with his one beady black eye. My heart pounded and my mind raced. Surely the bear would aggressively claim and defend the fish—it was his food. I expected him to flatten his ears, pop his jaws, and perhaps charge to drive me off; or even kill me.

He stood motionless. No snarls, no woofs, no jaw popping; he was totally relaxed. Dropping to the ground, he walked to the fish and stood a second time, looking in my direction, as if thanking me for the gift of the fish.

As he lowered his head to eat, I dashed to the kayak and paddled away from the island. Grateful for the safety of the river, I glanced back, hoping to see him one last time, but he was gone. I never again saw the one-eyed bear that was so unafraid, and so trusting of me. He was at peace with me, and with his world.

Drifting toward my camp, the image of the bear, staring at me without fear or hostility, caused my arms and legs to tremble again. I thought about my video camera lying somewhere in the tall grass. Like Sitting Bull's vision, was the one-eyed bear a sign from the spirit world? If this was a sign, what did it mean?

That afternoon, although I was still fearful and nervous, I kayaked to the island with pepper spray and a pistol. It didn't feel like weapons were really necessary, as the bear had never been hostile—indeed, he had displayed a spirit of peace and coexistence.

After a short hunt, I found the video camera. The fish under the olive tree was gone, and the only sign of the bear were his tracks, sunk deep into the soft sand and heading back across the channel.

■ ■ ■

Late that night, after building a small campfire, I reviewed the amazing footage of my second meeting with a one-eyed bear. There had to be a connection between the two bears—lessons to learn, wisdom, or a sign— but I didn't know what it was.

Perhaps Sitting Bull had a shaman to help interpret his vision. Clergy might suggest the Bighorn bear was a peaceful messenger, bringing the gift of forgiveness to me for killing the Alaskan one-eyed bear seventeen years before. Perhaps it was the ancient teaching: forgiveness of self comes through forgiving others.

Gandhi, a man of peace and forgiveness, spoke of the strength and courage (spirit signs of the Bear) necessary for grieving victims to embrace their tormentors and forgive them. He taught that both the broken and their victims are healed by forgiveness. The reward of forgiveness is that hatred and resentment and darkness are exchanged for freedom to love others and to live in peace—the great hope for mankind, and the world.

Many wise people have spoken and written about the miraculous power of forgiveness. Desmond Tutu said, "Without forgiveness, there is no future." Marianne Williamson wrote, "The practice of forgiveness is our most important contribution to the healing of the world."

My two Native friends who suggested I go on a vision quest, asked their elders what the signs of the messenger bear meant. One interpretation was that the bear was saying, "Forgive yourself for killing me, I have forgiven you." The other teacher counseled, "You ended a bear's life. You respected that life, and honored his spirit. You have been forgiven for taking the bear's life. Pass the gift of forgiveness on, and you will be free to love yourself and others more fully: It is the way of the Great Spirit."

■ ■ ■

The last tiny blue flame of my campfire flickered, and then died. The starlight of Montana's big night sky reminded me of Sitting Bull's vision of pony soldiers falling upside down from the sky. I wondered if the Indians have forgiven Custer and the cavalry for attacking their village. Have the army, and white people, forgiven the Indians for killing and scalping their soldiers? The battle happened over 130 years ago, but the healing power of forgiveness is patient, and seems to never lose its potency. For me, the wait was seventeen years.

Two creatures faced each other on an island in the Bighorn River. A tormented and heartsick man stood in awe of a powerful, yet peaceful, one-eyed bear. The bear was a shining messenger from the spirit world, who arrived bringing forgiveness in exchange for an offering of fish.

Something deep within me had connected with the bear. As he stood in front of me, I became aware of his calm and serene nature. Perhaps it was compassion or a mutual honoring of spirits. Maybe it was humility expressing itself through an incredibly powerful animal toward a weak and frightened man. I can't be sure.

When standing on his hind legs, the bear had appeared more human-like than any animal I have ever encountered. His essence was peace. He touched a quiet place deep within my soul, the place in me where it feels like God resides. I was healed by the power of forgiveness, delivered to me by a bear sent from the spirit world.

Parts of my being that had been sleeping for years began to awaken in the presence of the bear. They have always been there, but have remained buried under my ego and my unquestioned beliefs. The bear was my teacher. Awakening the student is what good teachers do.

Another great teacher preached: "I am the light of the world, and within you also is the light of the world." I now believe that as human beings, the Great Spirit invites us to stand humbly before those who have harmed us, awakening their compassionate hearts with the healing gift of forgiveness. And on it will go—from us, to them, to others, to all.

The bears seem to understand this, and soon—so shall we.

THE LAST DOG

*Half kneeling in a secluded bog, looking skyward into
the approaching darkness, he silently said goodbye.*

In 1860, *the U.S. Army rounded up Central Wisconsin Potawatomi Indians, who
refused to give up and leave their land, a special place that had been sacred to them for
many generations. The spirits of their relatives are there, and the place was their home
and connection to the Earth Mother and the Spirit World.*

*White Pidgeon, an old Potawatomi man, knew he would soon die. For a time, he
eluded the army, but eventually he too was herded onto a train, and relocated to "Indian
Country" in central Nebraska.*

*Without compass or map, White Pidgeon weaved his way through hostile white
settlements and walked 560 miles back to Wisconsin to die at his special place. White
Pidgeon's gravesite is a large circle of stones, which represents the connection and oneness
of all things.*

*Place was important to White Pidgeon. "The Last Dog," is a story about a white
man whose farm became a sacred and special place to him.*

■ ■ ■

Afternoon shadows slowly crept across the frozen bog. It was late
November in Wisconsin, and hope for an extended Indian summer disappeared with the arrival of snow flurries.

Robert Peterson ejected the still-warm shells from his worn but sturdy 20-gauge double-barreled shotgun.

"Here, Poppy. No bird," he muttered weakly.

It was the seventh flush and the easiest shot of the afternoon, but the game pocket in his faded canvas hunting coat remained featherless.

"Sorry old girl, you worked hard for that bird, but I just can't hit 'em anymore."

Poppy's tail trembled in high anticipation as she sat attentively, focused on the pocket of Robert's hunting coat. He turned the empty pocket inside out.

"Sorry, I'm plumb out of treats."

No retrieves, no treats, no grouse to sniff, but Poppy's eager eyes pleaded, "Let's keep hunting, boss. We'll get the next one for sure."

Time and place and circumstance vary, but in his heart, every hunter knows the final goodbye is coming. Robert's love affair with wild and beautiful places had sustained him through romantic heartbreak, family disruptions, and the death of loved ones. But arthritis, fading eyesight, and weakening muscles bring the reality of that final goodbye closer with each passing hunt. And that dreaded day had finally arrived for Robert Peterson.

Half kneeling in a secluded bog, looking skyward into the approaching darkness, he silently said goodbye to pheasants cackling at dawn on North Dakota prairies; goodbye to the satisfaction of a well-trained hunting dog proudly delivering a ruffed grouse to hand; goodbye to friends around a campfire with hunting stories to tell; goodbye to wild and beautiful places that made his spirit come alive, and that had enriched his life in so many ways.

The moon rose higher into the night sky. The old man patted his dog's head as they disappeared into the dark woods.

"Come on, girl. We've had a good run. Let's go home."

■ ■ ■

Robert and six different dogs had hunted together for over sixty years. Sam, Casey, Clancy Girl, Little Maggie, Cody Ann, and now Poppy—all had escaped with the boss man from loud and crazy people and places.

They had quietly slipped away from a hectic and angry society that was changing too fast. Woods and water had always soothed Robert's nerves and healed his tired spirit.

Robert's father taught him to eat everything you kill, waste nothing, try never to leave wounded game in the field, and always be thankful for the life of the animal that was taken. Robert, in partnership with his dogs, had always believed in, and hunted by, those standards.

On the night of Robert's last hunt, it was difficult for him to turn the key and drive to town. Poppy sat alertly in the passenger seat as the old man, exhausted from the walk out of the woods, coughed and gasped for air.

"Got another hunt in ya, ol' girl?" Robert grinned.

Poppy's ears raised, and her soft brown eyes seemed to say, "It's night-time, but you're the boss man. I just want to be where you are."

"Well then, let's go home and sleep by the wood-burning stove. This old man's done wore out."

■ ■ ■

For the next two years, Robert and Poppy only hunted from a duck blind close to the house. Richard, a young neighbor, had carefully and lovingly built the blind. Features included padded seats, an access ramp with hand-rails, and a blue-and-white "Handicap Accessible" sign that Robert had removed from an abandoned Exxon gas station.

During the duck season, Robert and Poppy spent hours in the blind watching the sky for ducks and geese.

"Poppy, sit! Here they come!" Robert would whisper just before pull-ing both triggers on the old 20-gauge shotgun.

"Missed again. Think I shot behind that one. You're such a good dog. We'll get the next one for sure!"

■ ■ ■

The woodstove creaked as it started to cool. Poppy groaned and stretched her legs toward the stove as the boss man scratched and lovingly stroked her soft ears.

"Hey, what's this?" Robert asked, feeling a grape-sized lump just below Poppy's right ear. "Maybe it's just a fatty tumor that old dogs get. At least I hope that's all it is."

Eight weeks later, after surgery, chemotherapy, and Robert's loving care, Poppy struggled to continue her life. She was ten years old, and her once-gleaming eyes had faded into a fixed, lifeless stare. Her breathing became shallow and erratic. Poppy and Robert knew their time together was coming to an end. Soon they too would have to say goodbye.

Poppy's strong and determined Labrador spirit drove her to wobble across the living room to be close with the boss man. Robert's gentle hand wandered over her old hip bones and protruding ribs as he lay with her sick and weakened body pressed against his.

"I'm glad we've had this time Poppy. Our love and spirits will be in our secret places forever. We've had a good run, Poppy. I love you."

For a brief moment, Poppy's breathing became more relaxed and peaceful, as tears streamed down the old man's leathery face. Poppy's body shuddered slightly, her legs stiffened, and in the darkness of that early morning, Poppy died.

Robert waited for a while before sliding Poppy's still-warm body onto a light blue sheet. He lovingly removed her leather collar. The letters and numbers on her brass name plate were worn smooth by years of hunting in the woods and fields.

Next to her head, the old man placed ribbons she had won—along with one of her favorite dog treats. While wrapping the sheet around Poppy and her worldly possessions, Robert again felt the prickly sting of tears coming to his eyes.

Robert had dug the hole for Poppy's grave over a year ago. The scrap of plywood covering the hole had faded, and it splintered into parched laminations as Robert pulled away the wood.

The old man leaned on the shovel and fondly remembered his first dog. Sam was a male black Lab, killed sixty years ago crossing a busy road for a conjugal visit with the neighbor's dog. After Sam, all of Robert's dogs were female yellow Labs. Casey's grave was in front of Robert, just to the left of Cedar Pond's Clancy Girl. Then, in a row, were the graves of Little Maggie, Heads-Up Cody Ann, and now, Poppy.

A lifetime of traveling and hunting companions, housemates, and best friends were at peace on the farm where they had played, hunted, and lain in the sunshine with the boss man. God was here, and to Robert, this place was sacred.

■ ■ ■

That fall, at the age of eighty-six, Robert hunted from the duck blind without a dog. Back pain required daily medication, and the arthritis in his right knee caused a limp. Keeping up with a Labrador tracking a running pheasant had not been a possible for nearly a decade. On the day of her death, Robert sadly realized that Poppy would be his last dog.

"I just can't love and lose another dog—I don't have the strength to do this again. And besides, a new puppy surely will outlive me."

Miraculously, Robert did knock down a few ducks that fall. Richard, his neighbor and hunting buddy, slapped hearty congratulations on the old man's back, and dutifully rowed the skiff to retrieve the ducks. Robert affectionately called his young friend "Ricky," and his help was much appreciated.

In the blind, Ricky and Robert talked about women, politics, and life; as well as playing thousands of hands of cribbage.

It always started with one of them shuffling the cards and asking, "You got a game in ya?"

For thirty years, Robert and Ricky hunted, laughed and cried together, raised dogs, and played cribbage. They had met at a meeting where alcoholics learn how to live without drinking. Once, Ricky told the group that years ago, his father had died after bar time while his car idled in a closed garage. This was before Ricky was born, and he grew up with only stories and pictures of his deceased father. In many ways, Robert was like the father Ricky never had, and Ricky was the son Robert never had. Over time, their connection had grown. They were in each other's lives—sometimes more, sometimes less—but there was always a deep and fundamental connection.

■ ■ ■

Robert Peterson was two months into his eighty-seventh year. His energy and mind were good, and most of his body parts functioned reasonably well—for a man of his vintage.

Robert answered his buzzing cell phone and heard Ricky's taunting cackle, "Hey old man, got a game in ya?"

"Of course I do. Bring your wallet and your dog. I'll take care of the rest."

It was a cold and gray February afternoon. Heat from the woodstove penetrated deep into Robert's joints and bones. During the first hand of cards, a sharp pain behind his right eye started to blur his vision.

"Fifteen two, fifteen four, and eight's a dozen," Robert counted tentatively, fumbling to grasp the peg and mark his score on the cribbage board.

"Yeah, right, and I've got 29," Ricky smirked, slapping the old man's trembling left hand.

"I thought the six was an eight. Just how many points do I have?"

"You've got a grand total of five, old man. Do you need a nap?"

"Something's wrong buddy. Seriously, I can barely see the board. My left arm feels dough—I mean dead."

Looking into Robert's confused and panicking eyes, Ricky blurted, "You're having a damned stroke! I'll call 911."

■ ■ ■

With closed eyes, Robert rested in his worn and faded green reclining chair. He could feel the warmth from the woodstove on the bottom of his right foot, but it was as if his left foot wasn't there.

Ricky called family and friends using the directory in Robert's cell phone.

Robert heard Ricky ask someone, "Do you know who has the medical power of attorney?" He told others, "He's resting now and can't talk. He'll be in the hospital soon."

Without the use of his left arm, Robert struggled to shift his position in the recliner. He felt Ricky's hand on his shoulder, and heard his reassuring voice say, "Hang on old man. The EMTs are almost here."

And then Robert Peterson's world started to darken and become silent as he drifted to a faraway place. In his dream, he moved in slow motion, swaying with the rhythm of North Dakota prairie grass. In the distance, near the end of the field, he saw a pack of Labradors hunting hard and urgently looking back, anxious for the boss man to come with his double-barreled 20-gauge.

His legs felt heavy; struggling to run through the thick Indian grass and little bluestem that tangled around his feet. Sweating and exhausted, almost within shooting range, the lead dog went on a familiar and rigid point. It was Cody Ann! Then Sam, the only black dog, Casey, Little Maggie, and Clancy Girl turned upwind into Cody's point for the flush.

The big pheasant finally flew. With dogs jumping and snapping at the rooster's dangling tail feathers, Robert pulled the first trigger, cartwheeling the rooster into a long, arcing fall.

"Fetch 'im up! Good dogs!" he yelled with a proud smile.

Smoke still curled from the first barrel. On the edge of the field, by a broken-down fence, he spotted another dog on point.

"My God, it's Poppy," he whispered as a second big rooster cackled skyward, crumpling with the shot from the second barrel.

"Hello Robert, can you hear me? My name is Dr. Shanahan. You've had a stroke. You're in the hospital."

"Hey buddy, it's me, Ricky. Got a game in ya?"

"Got doo burd down. Clancy find 'im" Robert mumbled through the respirator mask.

"Richard, did you understand that?"

"Ya, doc. He thinks he's hunting with his dogs. He'll need to rest and have coffee with cream when he gets back to the truck."

"I'll be damned old man, you do got another game in ya!" whispered Ricky.

■ ■ ■

After eight days of recovery in the hospital, Robert had been taken to an inpatient rehabilitation center. His mind was sharp, and after six weeks of working hard with a therapist, his speech returned.

He had lost ninety percent of the function in his left arm and leg. Walking and performing necessary daily tasks were difficult, if not impossible. After sixty days in rehab, since his left side was not responding to therapy, Robert was placed for permanent residency in Sylvan Crossing, a long-term care nursing facility.

An attractive young receptionist named Tiffany, wearing a revealing blouse and tight-fitting black slacks, welcomed Robert to Sylvan Crossing with a big smile.

"Hello Mr. Peterson. You'll be in room 116. I'll be down later to see if you need anything,"

"Wait till Ricky sees Tiffany," thought Robert. "He'll be up to visit me every day!"

■ ■ ■

Robert spent most of his time idly gazing out the window at traffic and people. The view across the street was blocked by a high-rise office complex and an upscale condominium project. To him, the scene was bleak and disheartening.

Sometimes the old man would look away and close his eyes to better remember his home. He could see sunlight dancing off the surface of Red Cedar Lake and brilliant yellow-and-red fall colors of the three big oaks growing near to where his dogs were buried.

Recalling the serenity and beauty of his farm, located only 20 miles away, often depressed him. Robert Peterson was homesick. Purpose and passion were leaving his life, and he was gripped with the fear of becoming like people in the hallways sleeping awkwardly in their wheelchairs.

His melancholy was often interrupted by a nursing assistant asking diminishing questions like, "How are we doing this morning, Mr. Peterson? We're having roast beef and mashed potatoes for lunch today. Do we like roast beef?"

"I like bluegill fillets and wild asparagus, or deer heart with fried onions," Robert might reply. But often, he just stared back, and said nothing.

In just three years, the old man had lost his ability to participate in his life passion—hunting the marshes and woods with his beloved dogs. Poppy died, and there was no hope of getting another dog. Gone was his freedom, and feeling of self-respect and dignity. He missed his farm—the place he loved—and he was losing the will to stay alive in a desolate and alien place called Sylvan Crossing.

■ ■ ■

Robert sat in the reception area, silently watching the tropical fish in the aquarium. An angelfish hung motionless and suspended near a bubbling aerator. The old man and the angelfish stared at each other, each carefully scrutinizing the creature on the other side of the glass. Mesmerized by the bubbles and the fish, Robert leaned back into his comfortable chair and closed his eyes to think. He contemplated whether his life was more fulfilling than the angelfish's, and which one of them had more freedom.

His partially paralyzed body and weary mind were inexorably slipping into the abyss of depression. His attorney had just left the reception area after Robert had reluctantly signed a contract authorizing Countrywide Auctions, Inc. to sell his personal property that was still on the farm. The lawyer had strenuously encouraged his client to also sign a Century 21 listing agreement for the sale of his home, farm buildings, and fifty-two acres of land.

"My dogs are buried there. I can't sell my dogs. Some doctor or rich lawyer, like you, might dig 'em up and build a big, stinkin', ugly house on their graves."

"Someday that will happen anyway," Robert's attorney patiently counseled.

"Well, dammit, that day ain't today, so leave me alone!"

■ ■ ■

A day pass, issued by Sylvan Crossing's nurse supervisor, protruded from the pocket of Robert's red flannel shirt. The clock with oversized numbers, let him know that it was 11:22 a.m.

"Where the hell is Ricky?" Robert muttered to himself. "The auction starts at noon. Bet that pup's been on another computer date and overslept again."

It was past noon when Ricky pushed Robert past the reception desk.

"Hello, Richard," Tiffany said with casual disinterest.

She ran to give Robert a long goodbye hug.

"I'll be thinking about you this afternoon Mr. Peterson. Good luck!"

"What's up with you and Tiffany?" Ricky asked while struggling to maneuver the old man into the passenger side of his pickup truck. "I've been hitting on her for six months, and she won't even look at me."

"I taught you how to shoot a shotgun; someday, I'll teach you how to talk to a woman like Tiffany. Let's go. The auction's already started."

He was silent as they drove past bucolic farms and woodlots on their way to his home. Finally, Robert opened up.

"Ricky, when I die, will you put some of my ashes in Red Cedar Lake, and the rest with my dogs?"

"Of course I will, count on me for that. But you're not dying anytime soon—I don't think you know how to do that!"

"Thanks, buddy. That gives me some peace. Yes—that gives me peace."

■ ■ ■

Nobody had lived on the farm since Robert's stroke. His grandmother's aluminum rocking chair was still on the front porch, the woodpile survived the winter without losing a log, and spiderwebs occupied corners of the windows and doors.

Now, on the day of the auction, over a hundred cars and trucks and trailers had found parking places in the yard, the driveway, and along the town road. Bargain hunters roamed curiously in and around the deserted home and farm buildings, anxious to bid on items that were important in Robert's life, before his stroke.

"Am I the only one who's ever had an estate sale before they're dead?"

Ricky shrugged at the question as his eyes intently followed a blond ponytail and tight blue jeans around the corner of Robert's garage.

"Let's park by the garage," Ricky suggested, pulling up next to a monster truck.

The young woman with the ponytail and tight jeans was struggling to get onto the elevated running board, and Ricky watched with intrigue.

"Would ya?" he asked the old man in a tantalizing tone.

"You're a sick and incorrigible horn dog, Ricky! Now go tell her boyfriend—the guy in the driver's seat—that I want to talk with him."

The ponytail's boyfriend, or young husband, boldly approached Robert. Bristling with annoyance, he poked his head through the open window.

"Yeah, what's up?"

Robert could smell the stink of alcohol and smoke on the young man.

Looking directly into the boy's glaring eyes, he calmly noted, "The left front wheel and left rear wheel of your truck are parked on Maggie's grave and Casey's grave. Please park you truck elsewhere."

"And if I don't?"

"Then I'll have my boy Ricky here hook a chain to the Allis Chalmers tractor and tow your truck to the dump—where it belongs."

Ricky stood in front of his truck with folded arms. Bemused, he watched the surprised and bewildered young man pull himself up into the monster truck's cab and park in a distant field.

Robert was excited, and eager for his young friend to push his wheelchair to where the auction was happening.

"Let's go and see how much money I'm making!"

The crowd followed the auctioneer's truck to the barn, and Ricky and Robert followed close behind the ponytail and her man. The auctioneer described the next item up for bid as "A pile of dog equipment: bowls, water dishes, training stuff, and old leather collars with brass name plates."

He asked for an opening bid of five dollars, then four, and finally, at three dollars the driver of the monster truck yelled, "Yup."

"That jerk's getting all the dog stuff for three dollars," Ricky groaned with disgust.

"Not today, he's not. Five Dollars!" Robert yelled, looking directly at the young bidder.

The auctioneer pleaded for six dollars, and Robert tauntingly bid ten.

"Twenty dollars," countered the boy.

The crowd watched, amused, as the pair dueled for the dog equipment and the worn-out dog collars.

"Thirty-five," Robert shot back, waving his strong right arm defiantly in the air.

The girl with the ponytail frantically signaled thumbs down to the auctioneer.

But, arching his back with a fist pump, her young warrior bellowed, "Fifty frickin' dollars!"

The auctioneer, unaware of Robert's stake in the expensive duel, tried to get the old man out of the escalating madness by quickly chanting, "Fifty dollars once, twice..."

"One hundred!" Robert shouted in a loud and perfectly clear voice. "One hundred dollars!"

Captivated, the crowd and auctioneer silently focused on the exasperated young bidder.

After a long pause, the defeated young man cursed, "Screw that old man," and stalked off toward his monster truck.

The ponytail worked her way through the crowd toward Robert's chair.

"I hope you're satisfied, grandpa," she sneered, spitting her words in cold disgust.

"The dog equipment for one hundred dollars to the man in the wheelchair. What's your number, sir?"

"Ricky, take my left hand," Robert grimaced as he raised his left arm.

Wobbly, but standing, Robert Peterson began to speak.

"That dog stuff belongs to the six best friends I've ever had—and they're all buried next to that garage. And in two weeks, my next best friend is arriving from Canada. She'll be seven weeks old, and I've already named her Rosie. She's related to Cody Ann, who's lying right over there."

An eerie hush spread through the crowd. The call of sandhill cranes erupted from the cattails near Robert's duck-hunting blind. Their ancient voices applauded the remarkable scene unfolding at the auction.

Standing, with both arms extending skyward, Robert proclaimed in a loud and clear voice, "It feels so good to be home! Thank you all for coming to my auction."

Dropping wearily into his wheelchair, Robert closed his eyes and listened to the auction crowd cheer.

"Ricky, I'm tired. Please take me into the house."

The auctioneer resumed his monotonous song, and the dusty crowd followed behind his slow-moving auction truck.

The last time Robert Peterson had sat in his green reclining chair, a blood vessel in the right hemisphere of his brain was hemorrhaging. He remembered the tranquil euphoria of his dream about hunting with his dogs. The healing sensations of freedom and connection and love for his dogs were powerful in the dream.

Ricky coaxed the woodstove to life, and questioned Robert about how he was able to find and put a down payment on Rosie. How and when did he regain the limited use of his left arm and leg, and how did he orchestrate all that happened at the auction?

"Tiffany did it all. At the risk of losing her job, Tiffany, day by day helped heal my broken body and regenerate my tired spirit. She's a beautiful young woman. I'll never forget her, and Ricky, I hope you don't either. She's worth the wait."

"You've had a long day Robert. How are you feeling?"

"I'm alive, I'm free, and I'm home. Go get the dog stuff; I can't wait for Rosie to get here."

"Think about it, Robert. You must know you won't outlive Rosie."

"No, I won't, but you will. And I know you'll be good to her. Tiffany assured me of that."

Robert lay back in the recliner, and closed his eyes.

"The auction's almost over. Take one hundred dollars out of my wallet and pay the auctioneer. And bring me a cup of coffee with cream," he yelled as Ricky walked out the door.

Heat from the woodstove warmed the bottoms of both feet. He was home at last, and Rosie would soon be here. Engulfed in peace and contentment, Robert drifted into a contemplative state. He remembered feeling profound sadness and loss the night he and Poppy walked out of the bog after their final grouse hunt. At the time, it felt like a death—the ending to an important part of who he was.

The old man began to feel a growing discomfort in the left side of his chest, and he used both arms to adjust and find a comfortable position in the recliner.

He recalled the wise words of his friend, Douglas C. Smith, who wrote in his book *The Tao of Dying*:

> *Why do we argue with what-has-been?*
> *Why do we fight what-is?*
> *Why do we try to control what-will-be?*
> *The practice of allowing reveals what is true.*
> *The practice of trying to control hides what is true.*

The loss of freedom and the dimming of his spirit in the controlling environment of Sylvan Crossing were indeed hiding the truth—Robert Peterson was not willing to await death warehoused in an expensive institution. In the midst of his illness, losses, and pain, he was coming closer to answering the question, "Who am I?" He needed more "allowing" and less "controlling" in his life, to discover healing truths to that ancient inquiry.

The burning in his chest had escalated, but Robert resisted the urge to call Ricky. He remembered his grief on the morning Poppy died. After burying her body, he made the decision that she would be his last dog. He would control pain by avoiding the risk of losing another dog. Besides, he surely would not outlive another dog—and who would take her hunting?

Why did he try to control "what-will-be"? Why did he fight "what-is"? Robert's gift of connecting with the Spirit of dogs helped bring forth his own truth, which had always been within him, but was disguised and hidden by shame and a hundred variations of fear. Why not practice allowing "what is true"? Rosie was on the way, coming from the East.

Robert had heard the calling and felt the need to be home; to complete the sacred circle of birth, life, death, and rebirth in the place he loved. A place that allowed him freedom to find his truth in the midst of loss, pain, and dying. Yes—the farm, his dogs, his home—this was the place, and now was the time—at last.

The crushing pain in his chest intensified, and was spreading to his neck and jaw. In his agony, Robert faintly heard the lonely music of a Lakota flute, and the steady roll of ceremonial drumming. Drawn to the rhythm of the drums and the sweetness of the music, he felt himself drifting toward the spirit world.

In the distance, he saw a warrior with a single eagle feather tied to his left braid. Seated between the three oaks, and the place where the dogs were buried, with raised arms, the Indian chanted the beautiful Native song of the dying.

It's time to break the pipe and say goodbye.
You are a friend of mine and I will surely miss you.
But this road I must travel on my own.
One silent eagle is flying toward the sunset.
Another one is soaring in the east.
And if you feel my Spirit in the snowfall,
You'll surely catch my scent in the summer rain.

Groaning and stretching his trembling legs toward the woodstove, Robert began to lose consciousness. It was as if he were in another part of the room, watching himself struggling to breathe, but content to allow the struggle to gradually play out.

Stillness and peace and love and pure whiteness filled the room—and Robert Peterson disappeared.

Ricky kicked the backdoor open with the side of his right foot.

"Hey old man, I've got your coffee with cream. Got a game in ya?"

Ricky looked for the microwave to re-heat their coffee, but it had been sold in the auction.

"Guess what? Got a call from the breeder, and we pick up Rosie at the airport tomorrow afternoon."

Coffee sloshed over the front of both Styrofoam cups as he stopped abruptly, staring at Robert's slumped and awkward position in the chair.

"Hey old man, wake up, here's your coffee with cream," Ricky said slowly with a hint of fear in his voice. "Rosie will be here tomorrow."

The woodstove creaked as it started to lose heat. Ricky found a folding chair that had survived the auction, and sat down next to his friend. The expression on Robert's face was one of peace and contentment, and the corners of his mouth revealed the smile of someone who had known happiness and joy.

"I'll keep my promise, Robert. You'll be one with Red Cedar Lake and with your dogs. Count on me for that."

Ricky took Robert's still-warm hand into his own. Lifting the limp hand to his lips, he kissed the worn and frail fingers that had dealt him so many cards, and moved the cribbage pegs so many times during their years together.

"Goodbye my friend."

Ricky gently placed Robert's 20-gauge double-barreled shotgun in his arms, and the old worn cribbage board in his left hand. He covered the old man's body with the gray woolen blanket that he and his dogs often slept on in front of the woodstove. Then Ricky buried his face in his hands and sobbed until there were no tears left.

■ ■ ■

A soft rain began to fall. Ricky pushed the back door open and stepped into the coolness of the night.

The wet grass in the yard glistened in the light slanting out of the kitchen window. The rain had cleansed the night air of the turmoil of the auction. He inhaled the scent. It was fresh and new and healing.

Ricky took the short walk to where the dogs were buried.

"Hello Sam and Casey and Clancy and Maggie and Cody Ann and Poppy. And hello Robert—I know you're here. Thank you for sharing your life with me. I will love and take care of your last dog, Rosie, in the same way you would have. And Robert, I'll be expecting some puppy training tips from you, and maybe even from Tiffany. Rosie will like that.

"I'm happy you lived your last day at home—the place you love. Tomorrow, your last dog, will be here. We'll come by so she can play in the grass and lay in the sunshine with all the dogs and you—the boss man.

"You are my friend, and I will surely miss you. Welcome home, Robert Peterson. You had a good run."

EPILOGUE: SIG VILAGI AND LEFTY

The stories in this book are true, in that the places are real and the events actually happened. The exception is "The Last Dog." Although the places and the characters are real, most of that story is about what sometimes happens in the lives of people who get old, and are unable to care for themselves or for their dogs. I have not yet reached that stage of life. But the true story that follows is about a good friend who is living that part of his journey, and how he and Lefty, his three-year-old yellow Lab, came into my life.

■ ■ ■

There never will be a last dog for Sig Vilagi. Soon after his most recent dog died, he bought a male yellow Lab named Lefty. The dog was one year old. Sig was ninety.

Sig has the gift of connecting with the Spirit of a dog. When two sentient beings connect with each other, differences in age or life expectancy shouldn't keep them from being in each other's lives. And Sig and Lefty were doing just that—until Sig broke his hip.

Sig Vilagi and I have known each other, and trained dogs at the Madison Retriever Club for over thirty years. In many ways, Sig has become like the many Labrador retrievers he has owned and trained for most of his ninety-three years of life. People who know him describe Sig as a kind and intelligent man, and a loyal and helpful friend—just like his dogs.

In addition, he's just a really good guy who laughs a lot and insists on enjoying life. His positive energy always lifts my spirits, and I'm grateful he's in this world and in my life.

Over the thirty-five years we've known each other, Sig and I hunted ducks together only once.

Two hours before daylight, in a harvested wheat field near North Dakota's Canadian border, my hunting buddy Craig Schlender and I sat on the tailgate of my truck sipping hot coffee, waiting for morning to arrive. The decoys were set, the layout blinds were in place, and the dogs were aired and ready to retrieve some ducks.

A pickup truck pulling a large white trailer turned into the field and headed toward my truck. A stocky young man, followed by his black Lab, jumped from the driver's seat and walked with an air of authority toward Craig and me.

"I think he's upset about something" whispered Craig.

"Who said you guys could hunt this field?"

"We got permission from Mrs. Jensen last evening," I replied, trying to sound friendly.

"Well I got permission from her husband yesterday noon, so you boys best leave right now!"

"We got here first and we're all set up," Craig shot back with some heat rising in his voice.

Spotting my Wisconsin license plate, the guide softened a bit.

"I got three hunters from Madison, Wisconsin in the truck. One of the guys who trains retrievers, traded me Tiger here for a three-day guided hunt. I've got to put birds in front of them—Tiger's a national champion retriever of some sort."

In the darkness, neither Craig nor the guide could see the smile spreading across my face. It couldn't be—but it just had to be—Sig Vilagi sitting in the passenger seat of the guide's truck. I had trained with Sig and Tiger. To many hunters, Tiger might even seem like a world-champion retriever, but by Sig's standards, he was just another field trial washout.

As I approached the truck, the automatic window descended, and I could make out the three hunters sitting in silence, staring straight ahead.

"You boys up for huntin' a different field?"

"That's up to our guide," Sig responded flatly.

"By the way, when did Tiger become a national champion?"

Shining his flashlight through the open window onto my face, Sig turned to the two hunters in the back seat.

"I know this guy! This is one in a million. I can't believe this!"

So we all hunted in the same field, everybody shot their limit of ducks, and Tiger retrieved like a national champion.

A few years later, I attended Sig's ninetieth birthday party. He told me he had just gotten a young male yellow Lab. I invited him to train with our group, and I gasped when we exchanged phone numbers.

"This is one in a million; I can't believe this!" I stammered. "Our phone numbers are identical, except that mine ends in three, and yours ends in four."

Were these events just coincidences I wondered, or were they signs of something more to come?

While I was finishing writing this book, my yellow Lab, Heads-Up Cody Ann MH, turned twelve. That's eighty-four on the human actuarial life expectancy table. Friends and dog-training partners began to ask if it was time for me to look for a new puppy.

My answer to that question always has been, and still is: "No, I don't look for a new dog; they seem to have a way of finding me."

One morning in November 2016, my cell phone rang. I recognized the number; it was one digit different from mine.

"Hi Howard, it's Sig. Did you hear that I broke my hip about seven months ago? I'm in assisted living. Lefty's happy at Full Throttle Kennel near Milwaukee, but boarding is expensive. If I do go home, it will be impossible for me to care for Lefty. He's a good dog, and deserves better than living in a kennel."

"I hope your hip heals, Sig, and I'm sorry that Lefty's been in a kennel for such a long time. What do you have in mind?"

"How about you and I go fifty-fifty and co-own Lefty? You finish him up with a Master Hunter title, and maybe we'll breed him. He's such a great marking dog, and he runs as hard and straight as any dog I've ever owned. And besides, I need a dog in my life, and I know you'll be good to our dog. Think about it."

The woman who owned the kennel loved Lefty, and was sorry to see him go.

"He's got a great pedigree, and it shows when he's working. He gets along well with the other dogs, and he's always happy—and you'll be happy with Lefty as well."

She and Sig were both right. I'm more than happy with Lefty, and he is now officially a Master Hunter in the AKC register. And if Lefty sires a litter, I know exactly where my next dog is coming from.

If we're not training or running hunt tests, Lefty and I visit Sig at the assisted living facility as often as we can. Aides there have told me that petting Lefty is the high point of the week for some residents. His presence encourages them to talk, often with tears in their eyes, about the dogs they had in their lives, sometimes eighty and ninety years ago. His tail never stops wagging, and he's especially fond of the residents and aides who occasionally slip him a treat.

Being a humble and unassuming man, Sig never speaks of the accomplishments and success he had in the field trial world. But Larry Johnson, one of his longtime training friends, has filled me in on some amazing facts about Sig that I never knew.

Sig Vilagi was inducted into the Retriever Hall of Fame in 2003. He judged over one hundred all-age field trial stakes, and was selected to judge the 1976 National Amateur Field Trial. He qualified dogs for five all-age Amateur National Stakes, two American Nationals, two Canadian Nationals, and was a finalist in both the Canadian and American Nationals.

Some notable dogs that Sig trained and handled include Aerco's Bit O'Honey, Le Coup de Grace, and Hillocks Spice.

I have learned much about dogs and dog training from Sig. When Lefty and I are running in a Master Hunt Test, I'll call to let him know what the test setups are, and how Lefty and I are doing. Often, Sig will give us encouragement and some handling tips like "just point him toward the bird and let him go—he'll find it." Then with a chuckle he might say, "I've got ESPN on, I'll watch for you guys." When we go to the line, there's Lefty, Sig, and me. I'm honored to be part of the team.

■ ■ ■

There really never has to be a last dog. Why try to control the future? If you love a dog, or a person, and they love you, does it really matter who dies first? The love will always endure. In the story "The Last Dog," Robert Peterson learned that. At the age of ninety, Sig Vilagi knew it. And now, so do I.